INTERNATIONAL COUNTERURBANIZATION

International Counterurbanization

British migrants in rural France

HENRY BULLER
Département de Géographie
Université de Paris VII

KEITH HOGGART
Department of Geography
King's College, London

Avebury

Aldershot · Brookfield USA · Hong Kong · Singapore · Sydney

© Henry Buller and Keith Hoggart 1994

Published by
Avebury
Ashgate Publishing Limited
Gower House
Croft Road
Aldershot
Hants GU11 3HR
England

Ashgate Publishing Company
Old Post Road
Brookfield
Vermont 05036
USA

British Library Cataloguing in Publication Data

Buller, Henry
    International Counterurbanization:
    British Migrants in Rural France
    I. Title II. Hoggart, Keith
    304.80941

ISBN 1 85628 508 1

Printed and Bound in Great Britain by
Athenaeum Press Ltd, Newcastle upon Tyne.

Contents

Figures

Tables

Acknowledgements

The research on which this book is based was funded by the Economic and Social Research Council under grant R000 23 3138 : 'La nouvelle vague: British house purchases in France'. We should like to thank the various officers of the Council who have assisted us at various points in our work, along with the reviewers and referees for this project who generously gave the nod that allowed the work to be undertaken. Apart from our own efforts in collecting and analyzing the data, we must acknowledge the efforts of our two interviewers, Amanda Milligan and Kris Wischenkämper, who put up with the frustrations and fatigue that accompanies long days of interviewing with remarkable cheer, accompanied by considerable effort and high quality work. For data entry we were well served by Wu Kegang and He Ludi, who deserve special mention for the speed and accuracy of their work. As with so much of our work, Roma Beaumont and Gordon Reynell deserve praise for the fine quality of their cartographic work, along with putting up with tense nerves as Keith's visits are regularly accompanied by abuse directed at machinery, himself and anything else that is passing, plus the fear that their super charged Macintosh will disintegrate in his hands.

We have incurred many debts of gratitude from the numerous British and French nationals that helped us undertake this research. For permission to draw up our initial data set, and for much subsequent help and advice, we thank the directors and staff of the SAFERs of Basse Normandie and Aquitaine-Périgord; in particular Messers Husson and Gaumer from these two bodies. Michael Mills was an early and much valued source of information, as were staff at the Direction Régionale de l'Equipement de Basse Normandie. In addition, we should like to thank the President and Monsieur Denis of the Chambre Interdépartementale des Notaires de Paris for their assistance in moving us towards obtaining a data set on foreign acquisitions of French residential property. Friends and colleagues within French academia, often amused by the arrival in their midst of one particular Briton in France, have provided us with many useful anecdotes and sources of information. We thank particularly Françoise Cribier of the CNRS for her valuable insights into migration patterns and Pierre Lenormand for readily sharing with us his considerable expertise on rural France and his knowledge of often exclusive data sets. Too many interviewees and questionnaire respondents went far beyond simply responding to questions, by inviting us and our interviewers to share meals, go to the opera with them, stay the week, use the pool, compare notes or give advice. In return for invading their privacy our efforts seem minor, but we trust that some satisfaction was gained from our responses to requests to ring the gas company to settle an outstanding bill, check the planning zone for a neighbouring land plot and so on. In all, we have to thank 406 British property owning households that completed a questionnaire for us in five départements in France. They have provided the empirical base on which much of this research is based. Apart from thanking them for their kindness and efforts, we wish them all 'bonne chance'.

Finally, as we have done in the past, we thank each other. Despite postal strikes, temperamental fax machines and unreadable discs, and even after various mutterings, exclamations and differences of interpretation, we still find it easy to talk to one another, laugh with and at one another, and even plan our next project together.

Henry Buller
Université de Paris VII

Keith Hoggart
King's College London

1   International counterurbanization

Over recent decades the countries that now make up the European
Community have experienced substantial change in their patterns of
international migration. In the 1950s and 1960s, the prevailing trend was of
movement from southern Europe northwards. With France and Germany as
the key reception points, the driving force for the governments of these north
European nations was to tackle structural problems of labour shortage
through mass immigration (Salt and Clout, 1976). For France the
importance of these flows was apparent in the government's willingness not
simply to ignore clandestine movement (Buechler, 1987), but even to
regularize it, with 1948-1981 seeing 1.4 million illegal immigrants benefiting
from amnesties that gave them the legal right to remain in France (Plender,
1988). In the 1970s, and more particularly in the 1980s, the south to north
pattern of European migration changed. The oil crises of the 1970s were key
prompts, as they reduced the need for imported labour and lessened
potential economic returns for those migrants who stayed. But political
change also made an impression, with shifts to democracy in Portugal and
Spain, which heralded membership of the European Community, along with
improved economic prospects at home, diluting the impetus to leave (King
and Rybaczuk, 1993). So, when growth in north European economies again
gathered pace, sources of imported labour were more dispersed and relied
more on nations outside the EC (Zlotnik, 1992). It is no surprise, then, that
recent research on international migration to EC member states has focused
less on labour demand and more on return migration, refugees and, more
recently, moves by highly skilled professionals (Salt, 1986; Findlay and
Gould, 1987). Yet international migration still involves significant movement
within the EC. Moreover, in character these cross border moves are taking
on new forms, that generate new geographical distributions. This book seeks
to explore one strand of these new movements, by examining the acquisition
of French homes by British citizens. An exploration of links between Britain
and France typifies new trends in European migration in two ways. On the
one hand, the focus on British households is novel, as the British previously
took very little part in international migration streams within Europe
(Zlotnik, 1992). On the other hand, these flows offer a new experience for

1

France, for although this nation houses a large immigrant population, its established migration streams have been city bound and manual labourer dominated (Ogden, 1989). British immigrants, by contrast, are predominantly middle class in occupation and rural in destination.

That general changes are occurring in the composition of the EC population in France is apparent from the declining importance of work related inflows. According to the OECD (1992), for instance, whereas more than half of all migrants from the EC came to France for work purposes in the mid 1980s, by 1990 the figure was little more than a third. If Fielding (1993) accurately captures the flavour of earlier decades by portraying international migration as Fordist, in that its emphasis was on satisfying the labour demands of mass production systems, then the decline of work related moves is perhaps symbolic of a shift toward post-Fordism; with its stress on constrained individuality and consumer preference. Examination of the changing foreign population of France certainly hints in this direction. With the exception of Portugal, whose government continues to pursue a low wage economic strategy that stimulates foreign job searches (Brassloff, 1993), inflows into France from the EC are now dominated by north Europeans; many of whom are not economically active (Table 1.1). Certainly, the number of northern Europeans is still small in absolute terms and their inflow is paid scant attention in mainstream writings on French immigration (e.g. Amar and Milza, 1990; Silverman, 1992). But this is not surprising if comparisons are made with more than 600,000 Portuguese residents in France, or the equally impressive Algerian and Moroccan numbers (Zlotnik, 1992). Yet, amongst European Community members, some convergence in populations is occurring. Thus, Portugal excepted, not only are absolute and relative rates of new arrivals from southern Europe much smaller than in the past, but their absolute representation in the French population is falling. Thus, apart for Luxembourg's 8.0 per cent fall, all the north European EC countries increased their population numbers in France between 1982 and 1990, whereas falls were recorded for each of Portugal (15.3 per cent), Greece (22.0 per cent), Italy (25.7 per cent) and Spain (34.0 per cent). Of course, some of this decline was due to naturalization and the acquisition of citizenship through marriage (Boisvert, 1987; Campani et al., 1987). Yet return migration is also influential, as studies of Mediterranean lands demonstrate (e.g. King et al., 1985; Cazarla Pérez, 1989). Moreover, the trend toward higher emigration from northern Europe, which is often for reasons other than work, seems to be increasing generally, with British retirement migration to Spain as one obvious example (Paniagua Mazorra, 1991; Valero Escandell, 1992).

Conceptualizing international migration

The problem that analysts face in seeking to understand and interpret these new migration patterns is that they have not gone far in developing a conceptual and theoretical armoury that is appropriate for the task. As Kritz and Zlotnik (1992) indicate, theoretical ideas and approaches to international migration are steeped in a mould that helps us understand permanent

Table 1.1   **The EC population in France in 1990**

| Nation | Arrivals since 1982 | | Total resident population | | % arrivals since 1982 that are economically active |
	Number	% EC total	Number	% arrived since 1982	
Belgium	20 029	12.7	56 129	35.7	49.0
Britain	28 359	18.0	50 422	56.2	50.7
Denmark	2 264	1.4	3 544	63.9	52.1
Germany	23 158	14.6	52 723	43.9	50.0
Greece	2 686	1.7	6 091	44.1	34.2
Ireland	2 274	1.4	3 542	64.2	63.4
Italy	16 040	10.2	252 759	6.3	55.2
Luxembourg	1 352	0.9	3 040	44.5	38.8
Netherlands	7 868	5.0	17 881	44.0	49.2
Portugal	41 972	26.6	649 714	6.5	58.6
Spain	11 559	7.3	216 047	5.4	45.5
EC total	157 561	100.0	1 311 892	12.0	52.4

Source: INSEE (1992)

relocations to Australia, New Zealand or the New World, but falls short in guiding us through the intermingling of international economic inter-dependence and the increasingly temporary nature of many migrant moves. Part of the problem is the recent nature of much work on international migration (Salt, 1986). A further problem is that the concepts, theories and even the issues studied for intra-national tend to be distinct from those examined for international migration (Salt and Kitching, 1992). At the same time, by the very fact that it involves more than one nation, research on international migration encounters problems of data incompatibility, with inadequacies in reporting being heightened by clandestine movements and by temporary or circulatory migrant profiles (White, 1986). For moves by north Europeans within the EC, our understanding is further limited because the focus of most international migration research is on labour flows, return migration and refugees (Salt, 1986).

Put simply, if much of the increased north European presence in France is consumption oriented, then traditional approaches to analyzing international migration offer little in explaining their pattern. Already we have evidence that issues of consumption are significant in new European migration trends; as with Valero Escandell (1992, p.67) finding that the primary reason why foreign residents were attracted to the Spanish Province of Alicante was its climate, followed by its cheaper cost of living. The fact that 49 per cent of his interviewed respondents mentioned climate corresponds closely with surveys of British tourists in Spain (the British being the largest group of immigrants in Alicante), which report that the main motivation for a vacation in Spain for 51 per cent of British holiday makers is 'to take the sun' (Rodríguez Martínez, 1991, p.58). Feasibly, what we are seeing in a European context is a repetition of what Bedford (1992) reports for migration links between the Pacific Islands and Australia and New Zealand, and which Balán (1992) also records for Argentina and its neighbours; namely, a situation where future migrants first learn of a place's attractions through tourism or, when they are tourists, become attracted by local job prospects and extend their stay (perhaps illegally). In these examples, we see different mechanisms through which consumption activities become expressed in migration. Particularly for retired migrants in Spain, the consumption of tourism leads to a home relocation that is designed to intensify, lengthen and broaden the consumption experience. By contrast, for Pacific islanders and those moving to Argentina, what starts as a temporary tourist connection turns into a more enduring move that is driven by the quest for a better job or a higher income.

The dynamic and interactive nature of such moves require that analysts are sensitive to the character and temporal specificity of population flows between places. Of course, these alone are not enough. British residents have been taking holidays in Spain in significant numbers since the 1960s, yet the British population of Alicante only stood at 2,875 in 1981, yet it had risen to 11,535 by 1986 and to 17,682 by the end of 1988 (Valero Escandell, 1992). It follows that we cannot conceptualize migrant prompts as static. Whether prompts arise in a previous home locale (push) or in a reception area (pull), both are subject to short term change that significantly heightens the propensity to change a home location. Moreover, it is unlikely that international migration can be distinguished from intra-national moves, especially given that internal movement is a more common migration option; for this very fact poses the question, why does an internal move 'fail' to satisfy those who enter an international migrant stream? Viewed in an historical context, the answer to this question is often easier to spot, for the act of migration changes both losing and recipient areas; as recognized in the downward spiral of loses in services, self-confidence and innovation that accompanies continuing rural depopulation (Parr, 1966). Indeed, recognition of such dynamism in migration flows led Kritz and Zlotnik (1992) to stress the need for a more encompassing vision of international migration, where fluctuations in the conditions of sending and receiving areas are both a product of and a determinant of the character and volume of migrant flows; with the attractions of internal and external destinations simultaneously interacting with events in sender and potential recipient areas, at the same time as they stimulate a change in the attributes of migrants. Adopting the systems approach which Mabogunje (1970) proposed for analyzing rural-urban migration, stress on the temporal evolution and inter-connections of migrant streams is emphasized through attention to feedback mechanisms (remittances, information, returnees, etc.), which help explain how trickles become streams, as well as telling us about what stimulates new migrant

4

streams. In effect, in arguing that we need a stronger appreciation of the totality of migration systems, Mabogunje points to the need for deeper understanding of the networks that bind places together, plus more knowledge of the channels through which migration is stimulated and sustained.

The literature on international migration already offers some recognition of the importance of such networks, although researchers continue to argue that our understanding of such networks is insufficiently developed (Gurak and Caces, 1992). One illustration of a network effect is found in the distribution of West Indian migrants in London, with residents from different islands revealing their family and cultural affinities in geographical concentrations in distinct parts of the city (Peach, 1968); as well as in the tendency to be located in specific cities within Britain (e.g. Byron, 1993). This pattern is not so different from that recorded for Irish immigrants, with nineteenth century inflows of Welsh migrants to London demonstrating a similar spatial concentration (Jones, 1991). In this we see similarities between international and internal migration, with various studies of outmigration from the Appalachians to northern US cities identifying class differentiated ties between single origins and specific destinations (Schwarzweller and Brown, 1967). With networks of families and friends having an obvious importance in encouraging and directing the development of migration flows from southern to northern Europe in the 1950s and 1960s (e.g. Boisvert, 1987), we already know that kith and kin links are instrumental in promoting employment related international migration; although these are not the only networks that offer this facility, as seen in the career moves that skilled technicians make within single companies (Salt and Kitching, 1992). But the diverse character of migrant moves inevitably means that networks of similar character can lead to different motivations for movement. A clear example is given by Bielckus and associates (1972), whose investigation of second home owners in England and Wales found that friends and family were the most common channels through which purchasers identified their future (second) home; a tendency that Dunn (1979) also recorded for retirement migration in rural areas.

In a discussion on international migration, it might seem out of place to raise the spectre of second home ownership within a nation. However, the logic of our argument is that this is not so. Not only do we hold that a false separation is too easily made between intra-national and international migration but we also charge that an understanding of migration processes requires that we focus on the variety of links that bind places to each other. If we restrict our attention and, more significantly, our conceptualization of migration, to significant residential breaks with a previous place of residence, then we neglect significant features in the development of migration processes. Thus, studies of elderly migration in North America make it clear that, for many retired people, seasonal residence in distant but warmer locations has become a way of life rather than a step toward a new permanent residence (Sullivan, 1985; McHugh, 1990). Effectively, such movers are migrants, for while their winter residence is a second home, it is one that often consumes equal and perhaps even larger segments of their time than their 'first' home (with residence in these two locations often being undertaken in long blocs of time, rather than numerous short stays).

Moreover, in such movements we can see characteristic migratory intentions, as in the tendency for elderly moves to be directed by family linkages; which are powerful factors in encouraging those with no proximate family to make residential changes, as well as weakening such desires when family members are nearby (Longino, 1992). Family linkages also attract the elderly to particular locations, as when they move to be closer to their children (Warnes, 1986; Clark and Wolf, 1992) or seek to return to the place they lived in in their youth (Cribier, 1980).

Given that throughout much of Europe the strongest migrant channels in earlier decades were from rural to urban areas, this latter tendency has often resulted in a reverse urban to rural flow on retirement (Cribier, 1980; Rees, 1992). This highlights a further dimension of elderly migration, which is the importance of place amenity in home relocation decisions. We return then to the issue of consumption led migration; with counterurbanization within nations clearly revealing that this is not something that is restricted to the elderly (Perry et al., 1986; Cross, 1990). Yet consumption led moves can favour a different geography of destinations from those stimulated by employment motives; if only because substantial employment opportunities and occupational shortages tend to occur in a more constrained array of centres than the variety of consumption options that are available to households. Of course, there is always the question of why a move takes place at all. For, as with labour flows, if migrants choose to change their residential location, then generally we can expect that their target destination is believed to offer more than their existing base (Clark, 1986). For elderly migrants, climate and access to kith or kin are significant influences in this regard, with climate demonstrating its drawing power both in intra-national (Warnes, 1993) and in international flows (Valero Escandell, 1992). It comes as no surprise then to find assertions that the destinations of elderly migration are significantly influenced by previous holiday destinations (Warnes, 1991a; Cribier, 1993). Put in this context, the overseas destinations that British nationals choose for holidays provide one pointer to potential targets for British emigration (Table 1.2). With France and Spain so obviously ahead of other nations in this regard, it is pertinent to note that both these countries house significant British populations, whose numbers are rising rapidly. Thus, the French census records a jump in British numbers from 34,000 to 50,422 between 1982 and 1990, while Spain saw its numbers increase from 46,914 to 73,535 from 1986 to 1989 (Bel Adell, 1989, p.25; Valero Escandell, 1992, p.277).

Yet these figures are far from complete. For France, for instance, another measure of the British population is the possession of a *carte de séjour*, which is a residence permit that all foreigners require if they stay in France for more than three months at a time. Here the Ministère de l'Intérieur reported 50,954 British residents in France in 1989, with a continuing upward trend seeing this rise to 62,041 by 1991. That these figures are higher than those in the census is not a new phenomenon, for whereas the 1982 census reported 34,000 British residents, the Ministère de l'Intérieur placed the figure at just below 40,000 as early as 1980. Part of the reason for this is that holders of a *carte de séjour*, although regarded as long stay residents in France, need not be permanent residents there. They might divide their time between homes in Britain and France.

6

Table 1.2   Main destinations for British tourists in 1988

| Nation | Tourist arrivals | | British rank for number of tourist arrivals |
	Number	British as % of all foreign tourists	
France	6 645 000	17.4	2
Ireland	2 090 000	69.5	1
Italy	1 819 232	3.3	6
Malta	476 578	60.8	1
Portugal	1 064 571	16.1	2
Spain	7 645 598	14.1	2
USA	1 818 029	5.4	4

Source: World Tourism Organization (1990)

This brings us back to the link between second homes and migration. We have already seen that research in North America has identified a tendency for some elderly households to split their time between two homes, with residence in one being as significant as in the other (Sullivan, 1985; McHugh, 1990). In many instances such homes were not acquired as one step towards a change in first home location, yet there is little doubt that second home acquisition often does have this intention; as when a second home is purchased with a view to it becoming a permanent place of occupation on retirement (e.g. Bielckus et al., 1972). Moreover, even during periods of employment, second homes can attract significant segments of their owners' time; as Bollom (1978) indicated in a four district survey in Wales, where mean average occupancy rates ranged from 87 to 123 days a year. This is not meant to imply that second home ownership is identical to migration, for it is clear that many householders see their second residence as a short duration, temporary haven away from life's routines, and not as a step towards a new permanent home. However, recreation and tourism do provide a network connection that enhances the prospect of migration to particular (tourist) destinations. In this regard, second home ownership is a particularly strong tie with a potential migration destination. How exactly it is linked to more permanent changes in residential location is an empirical question. Certainly, given the very evident need to understand the processes that bind places to each other and that lead to international migration (Kritz and Zlotnik, 1992), we should examine whether second home residence acts as a vehicle through which more permanent residential changes occur.

Moving to France: the rural choice

At this point the reader will be justified in pointing out that we have provided limited backing for our argument that much north European migration to France is consumption driven. After all, the figures in Table 1.1 reveal that around half of all 'permanent' north European migrants are in employment, which might be assumed to be a very high percentage if we make allowance for household members who do not have paid employment, for children and for retired people. Yet the reality is far from this. Thus, if we examine the OECD continuous reporting system on international migration, we find that France has taken between 1,200 and 1,900 British workers in each year between 1983 and 1989 (OECD, 1992). Looking at 1987-1989, the numbers (in thousands) were 1.6, 1.6 and 1.8. Banque de France (annual) figures on net investment in non-commercial property by British nationals reveal a quite different pattern. Here, for the same three years, investment levels (in millions of French Francs) were 499, 564 and 1,524, respectively. Confirmation that this difference does not result simply from workers purchasing more expensive property is apparent from other sources. For instance, according to the Fédération Nationale des Agents Immobiliers, 2,000 British purchasers bought a home in France in 1987, which rose to 4,000 in 1988, to 14,000 in 1989, and was expected to be in the region of 20,000-25,000 in 1990 (Rueff, 1990). Such was the sense of expansion in British property purchases at this time that two property journalists claimed that 1992 would see 200,000 Britons having purchased a home in France (de Warren and Nollet, 1990). Other journalists went further, with Smithers (1991, p.38) asserting that more than 200,000 Britons had already been 'lured' into French 'second home ownership'.

The problem each of these writers faced, which is still with us today, is that there is no official register of British home owners in France. Indeed, many British householders who do own property there do not appear on any of the official counts that exist. This can happen for numerous reasons, including the fact that British home owners do not qualify for official registers (for instance, if they spend less than three months at their home they do not need a *carte de séjour*) or else they were not at their property when an official tabulation was taken. At the same time, whether through ignorance, an aversion of 'bureaucracy' or fears about tax status, some residents choose not to appear on these registers. Whatever the reason, the increase in British home ownership that property specialists and journalists have identified is significantly higher than official figures on 'permanent' British residence.

Moreover, one of the most striking aspects of this new British interest is its rural orientation. This we can see by examining two different measures of the British presence in France. The first is seen in changing patterns of long stay occupation, as revealed by British holders of a *carte de séjour*. At a regional level, the most evident aspect of this shift arises from the declining importance of the Paris region (Ile de France), which saw an increase in British residents of just 23.1 per cent between 1980 and 1991, compared with growth rates of more than 200 per cent for the traditionally

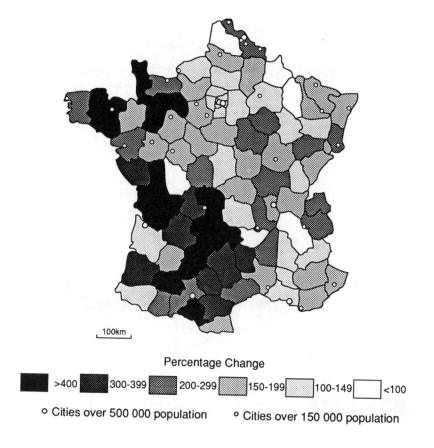

Percentage Change

>400 | 300-399 | 200-299 | 150-199 | 100-149 | <100

○ Cities over 500 000 population   ○ Cities over 150 000 population

Figure 1.1   Percentage change in the number of British *carte de séjour* holders by département, 1980-1991

agricultural regions of Bretagne, Limousin, Midi Pyrénées and Poitou-Charentes. Visually, for the départements of France, this preference for locations away from cities is striking (Figure 1.1). Our second indication finds voice in the recent upsurge in British buying activity, which encompasses both permanent and second home buyers. Here, we calculated for each département the percentage of all 1,054 French estate agents and notaires which we identified as having advertised French property for sale in Britain in 1991 and 1992 (Hoggart and Buller, 1992b). The logic of Figure 1.2 is that companies who wish to sell property are more likely to advertise if they believe that their local area attracts British buyer interest. Elsewhere we have examined the operations of French estate agencies and can confirm that their operations are localized (Buller and Hoggart, 1993);

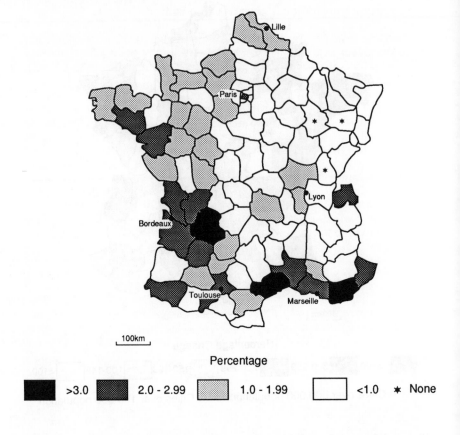

Percentage

■ >3.0 ▨ 2.0 - 2.99 ▨ 1.0 - 1.99 □ <1.0 ✳ None

Figure 1.2   **Percentage of all French companies advertising property for sale in Britain in 1991 and 1992, by département**

so a plot of office locations provides an accurate representation of where properties are offered for sale. Indeed, in France as in Britain, companies involved in this property market confirm that the overwhelming majority of British customers are intent upon purchasing a rural home (Hoggart and Buller, 1992a). More eye catching confirmation that rural residence is the focus of British attention is obtained by examining the pictures of properties for sale that make a regular appearance in magazines on French property that are published in Britain. Even a cursory look at journals like *French Property Buyer* or *Living France* brings this rural orientation home forcefully. Reinforcing this message are the materials and tone of articles in these magazines, as well as in the monthly *French Property News*.

Investigating international counterurbanization

The fact that British nationals are moving to rural parts of France might not strike the reader as peculiar in an age when urban to rural migration has effectively become the norm in north west Europe (Fielding, 1982). However, while research in Britain has shown that rural in-migration is stimulated by inflows associated with retirement, longer distance commuting and new job creation (Cross, 1990), if job related moves do have a limited role in international migration from north Europe to France, this raises the prospect that what we are seeing in British purchases of French property is little more than the combined effects of retirement migration and increased second home ownership. After all, within Britain, the geography of elderly migration (Grundy, 1987), and of second home purchases (Bielckus et al., 1972; Bollom, 1978), both show a deep attachment to rural and coastal environments. Yet even if these flows dominate British linkages to France, their potential impact on rural development could be considerable, as service expansion to cater for this new population should raise income opportunities for local residents (Perry et al., 1986). This is not simply on account of the goods and services that in-migrants buy, but also arises from the innovations they introduce. As Perry and associates (1986, p.212) explained:

> Once installed in the smaller settlements, middle class 'do gooders' pressurized effectively to develop a range of arts, crafts, welfare, educational and recreational amenities, that attracted more commuters from the bigger towns. The influence of individual actors upon the scene was thus not insignificant ...

Yet we cannot assume that such effects will occur automatically, for migration into rural areas is distinguished not only by the numbers involved but also by the selectivity of members of a migration stream (Lewis and Sherwood, 1991).

At this point we must state the obvious by pointing to the fact that the rural in-migrants that interest us are crossing an international boundary. This is not the same as long established British patterns of acquiring a second home or of changing a place of residence on retirement; both of which have involved property acquisitions in distant locations for some decades. Whether we look at Banque de France investment data, interview estate agents, undertake detailed local examinations of French land transaction records or refer to journalists' accounts, the picture that emerges is one of sharp increments since 1988 in the acquisition of French rural property by British nationals. There is an obvious issue of why such home relocations have been directed toward France rather than Britain, but theoretically this takes a more interesting form if we ask why the upsurge occurred at this precise point in time. Coincidentally, we should ask why this migrant stream has been directed so forcefully toward rural destinations.

When we examine the literature on elderly migration and on second home ownership we find suggestions that help us answer the second of these questions, but little that contributes to addressing the first. In fact, we hold that these literatures not only do not provide an answer to the temporal question but also do not satisfactorily account for movement into rural areas.

Principally, this is because the factors that lead to the procurement of a second residence or a retirement home are by-products of broader forces that instil in the British middle classes a strong desire for rural living (Thrift, 1987). What we seek to show in Chapter Two is how the depopulation of rural France generated a stock of dwellings that are ideally suited to meeting the imagined rural idyll of the British middle classes. Added to which, although much of rural France now sees a positive migration balance, this has barely touched the house stock which attracts British buyers. At the same time, we will show that the late 1980s produced a particular conjunction of forces within British housing markets that made it more difficult to acquire a rural home in Britain and made French home acquisition a cheap option. In Chapter Three we take this argument further, by examining other immigrant groups in France and particularly northern Europeans. Here we draw attention to the manner in which British buyers have sought areas that make their geographical distribution distinct from those of other nationalities.

In this we will be viewing migration as a dynamic system (Mabogunje, 1970; Kritz and Zlotnik, 1992), in which we need to understand the circumstances of the sending community, along with conditions in the recipient area. These constitute our focus in Chapter Two and in Chapter Three, with regard to both the temporal and the geographical circumstances of British home purchases. But to round off this picture we must focus on the development and evolving character of linkages between places that receive and send migrants. This we move onto in the fourth and fifth chapters. In Chapter Four the primary concern is with the selection of France, and specific areas in France, paying particular attention to the reasons for home purchase. What we develop here is an argument that draws out the peculiarities of British property buyers. Our argument is that much French property acquisition has been individually driven, with few ties of familiarity, or of nearby kith or kin, to sustain its momentum. Rather buyers have been drawn by an idealized image; what various authors have described as the rural idyll (e.g. Forsythe, 1980; Thrift, 1987). But for British buyer interest to be sustained and to have developed as it has, there has had to be positive feedback about the purity and 'reality' of this idealized rural world. After all, across the aggregate, if not for every individual, the middle classes have the skills and contacts to publicize any imperfections in this image. In Chapter Five the reasons for so positive an image are easily presented, for British owners have found that the idealization they brought with them has be matched by their experience of living in France. Moreover, the British 'invasion' of rural France has not, in their eyes, diminished the qualities they sought when they bought their home. As a consequence, they are well placed to present French property ownership in positive terms; thereby helping promote further interest amongst British nationals, as well as sustaining latent demand for French property ownership, even at the height of the current British recession.

2   The context of migration: British push and French pull

Whether on a sub-regional, national or international scale, migration implies that substantial differences exist between departure points, and the way of life led there, and migrant destinations. These may be differences of economic opportunity, of freedom from oppression or, more simply, of residential quality. To understand what attracts British home buyers to rural France, we should be clear about what pulls them toward this environment and, to place this migration stream in a broader context, appreciate how these features of the French countryside have evolved. At the same time, we should understand the character of those push factors which made investment in a British rural home seem less attractive than owning a French *maison de campagne*. In this chapter, we will argue that the factors that 'pull' British buyers to rural France are linked to its relative 'emptiness', which partly results from the dramatic population losses that the French countryside has experienced, which have not been compensated by urban to rural counterurbanization flows. As for the 'push' factors that orient buyers away from Britain, here the 'availability' and 'affordability' of rural properties are critical. How each of these features have provoked the development of migrant streams from Britain to France is explored in turn below.

Demographic decline in rural France

If Britain is a society with an essentially urban culture, then France, despite rapid urbanization which saw its urban population grow from 46 per cent in 1950 to 84 per cent in 1990, still has a culture that is deeply rural. Although more than three quarters of the French population live in urban areas (with 44.4 per cent in centres of 100,000 inhabitants or more), most French citizens are only a generation or two away from their rural origins (Bodiguel, 1986). Hence, the urban population is far closer to its rural counterpart than has been the case in Britain for more than a century. This closeness is founded upon sustained family ties with rural relatives and upon the retention of rural family properties by urban dwellers (often as second homes or later for retirement), as well as frequently being expressed in an enduring sense of possessing a rural origin. These personal ties with the countryside find obvious expression at the national level. For one, rural France has a high profile in academic and popular writings (e.g. Michelet, 1975; Hervieu, 1993). For another, as recent GATT negotiations have shown, French farmers benefit from broad support amongst the general populace and in government circles. This 'privileged' position is reinforced by the administrative divisions of France, which provide a strong rural representation, particularly in the second chamber of national government, the Senat (Boussard, 1990). There is of course a geographical basis to the importance of rural areas in France. Thus, while France has approximately the same population as Britain, it covers more than twice the surface area. Indeed, as well as incorporating north European, continental, alpine and Mediterranean climatic zones, it also contains a rich diversity of regions which are physically, historically and culturally distinct. Collectively, these factors suggest that there are major differences in the conception and role of the countryside in France and Britain (Lowe and Buller, 1990).

Yet a plethora of recent books and articles express a pervasive concern for the future of the French countryside (for a review, see Lowe and Bodiguel, 1990). In early works of this kind, large tracts of France were identified as becoming 'empty' as a result of outmigration (e.g. Bontron and Mathieu, 1977). That some of these regions were among the most prosperous agricultural areas (such as the Beauce), while others were among the poorest (the Ariège), has long confounded attempts to generalize about the future vocation of the French countryside (Béteille, 1981). Even so, two processes dominate this demographic decline; namely, agricultural modernization and the gradual urbanization of economic and social values. While some might see these processes as ubiquitous in advanced economies (Charrier, 1988), the French experience is somewhat distinct, particularly in comparison with Britain, both due to the tardiness with which such processes gained steam and in the profound impact they have had upon rural communities. In terms of their impact, what is particularly significant for this book is the manner in which demographic decline has made rural property available to outside buyers. In terms of British interest in French property, the attractions of rural dwellings are heightened by their socio-economic context, wherein low population densities, few economic alternatives to agriculture and a multiplicity of small, 'autonomous' villages, all contribute to a 'genuine' sense of rurality. It is precisely this aura of genuine rurality that many believe disappeared from the 'urbanized' countryside of lowland Britain some decades ago (Lowe et al., 1986).

Agricultural modernization

The modernization of French agriculture from the 1950s until the 1980s undoubtedly caused substantial decline in the farming population. Indeed, this modernization was essentially predicated upon the shedding of farm labour. A series of government Acts (notably the *Lois d'Orientation Agricole* of 1960 and 1962), along with various incentive schemes that have been introduced since the 1950s, encouraged both a general reduction in the agricultural labour force and the replacement of older farmers by their younger offspring. These policy measures, founded on a need to increase agricultural productivity, coincided with a process of evolutionary change

14

within the agricultural population. Initially isolated from the central thrust of (urban) social modernization, the farming population has increasingly been integrated into that modernization (Mendras, 1967; INSEE, 1993).

Yet while the agricultural population of France has been declining since around 1910, this decline only became precipitous after 1950. If the number of active farmers and farm workers numbered some 5,135,000 in 1954, or 26.8 per cent of the working population of France, by 1990 it was just 1,264,000 or 5.0 per cent of the working population (INSEE, 1993). This represents a rate of loss of 3-4 per cent per year, with the recent 1982-1990 period recording an annual loss of 4.9 per cent. Between the years 1954 and 1974, which are regarded as the golden years of the postwar agricultural revolution in France, the farming population fell by around 70 per cent (Alphandery et al., 1989). Most recently, and following the political events associated with the reform of the EC Common Agricultural Policy, commentators have suggested that if the logic of agricultural intensification and global commercialization continues, then the French agricultural population could fall to between 300,000 and 500,000 by the end of the century (Jacquot, 1992). Even without this, further decline is expected. For amongst those who have resisted the pull of employment in urban centres, the remaining farm population is relatively aged, despite a panoply of measures to aid younger farmers (Ministère de l'Agriculture, 1992). With a top heavy age structure, the farm sector lacks an assured succession of workers for the future; with current estimates pointing to 410,000 farmers having no successor in their immediate family (Guyotat, 1992).

Demographic upheaval has nonetheless been accompanied by substantial gains in agricultural productivity, as well as structural farm change. The issue of productivity gains is not one that directly concerns us here (for a classic review see Klatzmann, 1978), but three elements of structural transformation have had significant consequences for migration patterns; namely, the organization of farm land, the availability of farm buildings and the impact on land prices. It is true that the policy of rural land reorganization, which is widely known as *remembrement*, substantially predates post-1945 pressures for increased agricultural productivity. Nevertheless, the restructuring of farm holdings to create larger production units has been an integral part of farm modernization in recent decades. By December 1990, some 14 million hectares of agricultural land had been reallocated through land reorganization schemes; which represents almost half of all farm land in France. Indeed, while the total amount of land in farm production has not diminished greatly (from 33.4 million hectares in 1950 to 30.4 million in 1988), the number of farm holdings has fallen precipitously, from 2.2 million in 1955 to an estimated 924,000 today (Ministère de l'Agriculture, 1992).

While such reorganizations are significant for the impression they have made on the spatial organization of local agricultural landscapes, they also have bearing on British-French migration patterns in two important ways. On the one hand, agricultural modernization has assisted a process of regional specialization within French agriculture (Hervieu, 1993), which has provoked an intensification of the ancient division of France into a

15

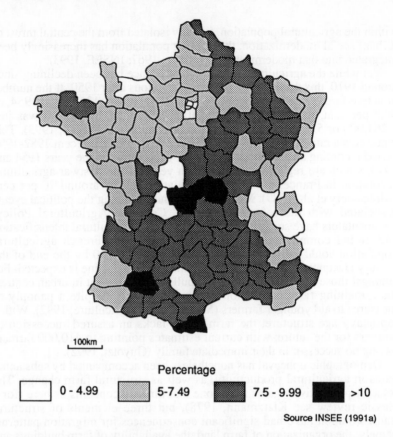

Percentage

| | 0 - 4.99 | | 5-7.49 | | 7.5 - 9.99 | | >10 |

Source INSEE (1991a)

Figure 2.1   **Vacant dwellings in 1990 as a percentage of the housing stock, by département**

broad central, north eastern and eastern sector of open field landscapes and a southern and western sector which is given over essentially to small fields and enclosed structures (Dion, 1981). The first of these area types has a long association with a highly productive, cereal based agricultural economy, which presents a virtually monofunctional rural landscape. The latter is far more heterogeneous, ranging from the rich husbandry zones of coastal Brittany to poor peasant farms in the south west, but this variety is not simply at a regional level. Within regions there is also a rich diversity of landscapes and rural communities have traditionally been multifunctional (Brunet, 1992). Significantly for migrant flows, the bocage type agricultural landscapes of western and southwestern France bear close parallels with the idealized image of 'the countryside' of so many British people (e.g. Young, 1988). As such, in so far as land reorganization is increasing the agricultural polarization of French rural space, it reinforces the differential

Table 2.1   **Percentage of second homes and vacant houses in the dwelling stock by commune size, 1990**

Commune population	Second homes as % of all dwellings	Vacant houses as % of all dwellings
Under 50	43.7	9.4
50 - 99	33.0	9.8
100 - 199	26.9	9.5
200 - 499	21.7	8.7
500 - 999	18.4	7.6
1 000 - 1 999	17.1	7.1
2 000 and over	18.6	6.3
All rural communes	19.9	7.8
France	10.7	7.1

Source: Derived from INSEE (1991b)

attractiveness of landscapes in the French countryside to British property buyers.

Also influential in attracting outside buyer interest is the availability of surplus farm land and buildings. Whatever the causes of declining farm numbers, where there are few economic alternatives to agriculture, the barns and stock buildings that are liberated through farm closure regularly find no other uses and remain idle. In the poorer rural regions, which include much of southern and western France, even surplus farm land is often not taken over by neighbouring farmers (SAFER, 1992). Vacant housing also results, with national figures pointing to 7.2 per cent of the total housing stock lying vacant in 1990 (INSEE, 1991a). [1] However, this national average masks considerable geographical variation (Figure 2.1), with strong biases both toward départements that are further away from major urban centres, such as those of the northern Massif Central and south west France (notably the départements of Allier, Creuse and the Gers - see Figure 2.2 - where the proportion of vacant dwellings exceeds 10 per cent of the housing stock) and that have lower population densities (Table 2.1). Rural exodus clearly lies behind the availability of vacant housing units, although the smaller number of vacant homes near cities owes much to urban residents acquiring or retaining more accessible properties as second homes (Clout, 1977). The uneven geography of vacant housing is further emphasized by speculative apartment construction in mountain and coastal zones, which results in built units remaining technically vacant for a considerable time before sale or lease (Bontron, 1989). Not surprisingly, the geography of vacant dwellings

Ile de France
1 Yvelines
2 Hauts de Seine
3 Paris
4 Val de Marne
5 Essonne
6 Seine et Marne
7 Seine St. Denis
8 Val d' Oise

100km

Figure 2.2 **The départements of mainland France**

18

has parallels in other features of local housing, with western France being characterized by relatively weak rates of new house building, particularly in rural communes (Troufleau, 1992), and by a relatively aged housing stock (Bontron, 1989).

A key consequence of land abandonment is declining agricultural land prices. In the same way, vacant housing, combined with the lack of local demand for an ageing housing stock, keeps house prices at a low level. Most certainly, compared with other EC nations, farm land is cheap in many parts of France (Figure 2.3), and particularly in those regions that lie distant from competitive land uses (i.e. beyond the hinterlands of the major urban conurbations and the coast). This combination of cheap prices and weak local demand results in the gradual removal of land from agriculture. Between 1989 and 1991, for instance, 212,200 hectares of farm land were acquired in each year by non-farmers, who today represent 39 per cent of all buyers of agricultural land (SCAFR, 1993a). Yet significant regional differences exist in land sales to non-farmers. These owe much to uneven demand for housing development (which is focused on urban hinterlands, and on coastal and mountain zones), but in some measure they also reflect new investment, which is attracted by the cheapness of property in inland rural zones. British and other north European buyers have played a notable part in sustaining this second trend. Yet it is not simply low prices that draw international migrants. The peculiar geography of agricultural modernization in France also reinforces regional differences in the availability of traditional rural dwellings, in house and land prices, and in the retention of highly varied agricultural landscapes.

Rural outmigration and urban expansion

Of course, farm modernization has not been the only factor that has helped produce this geography. While farmers and farm workers have been major contributors to rural population decline, their actions are just one component of the rural to urban population shift. Thus, whereas the rural population in 1946 numbered 17,600,000, by 1990 it was 14,717,000. While part of this demographic decline is explained by boundary and definition changes, [2] one cannot deny the precipitous loss of rural population during the postwar period. Certainly, this population decline has not been constant or ubiquitous, yet, although counterurbanization processes have come into play since the late 1960s or early 1970s, rural exodus is still a reality for many parts of France. Indeed, eastern départements in the Lorraine and Champagne Ardenne still display absolute rural population losses, while in the Centre region (from Aveyron to Nièvre) and in non-coastal western regions (from Charente to the Orne), rural exodus is not compensated by in-migration (Figure 2.4). Certain of these areas are traditional zones of rural exodus (Béteille, 1981) or have been left behind by agricultural modernization. Others are among the more productive agricultural regions, in which labour has been shed through increased mechanization (Gervais et al., 1977). Yet the fact that the dominant pattern of the postwar years has been for the least populated communes to experience greater depopulation than larger centres suggests that a minimum size exists for sustaining rural population which has changed by little over time (Table 2.2). That this

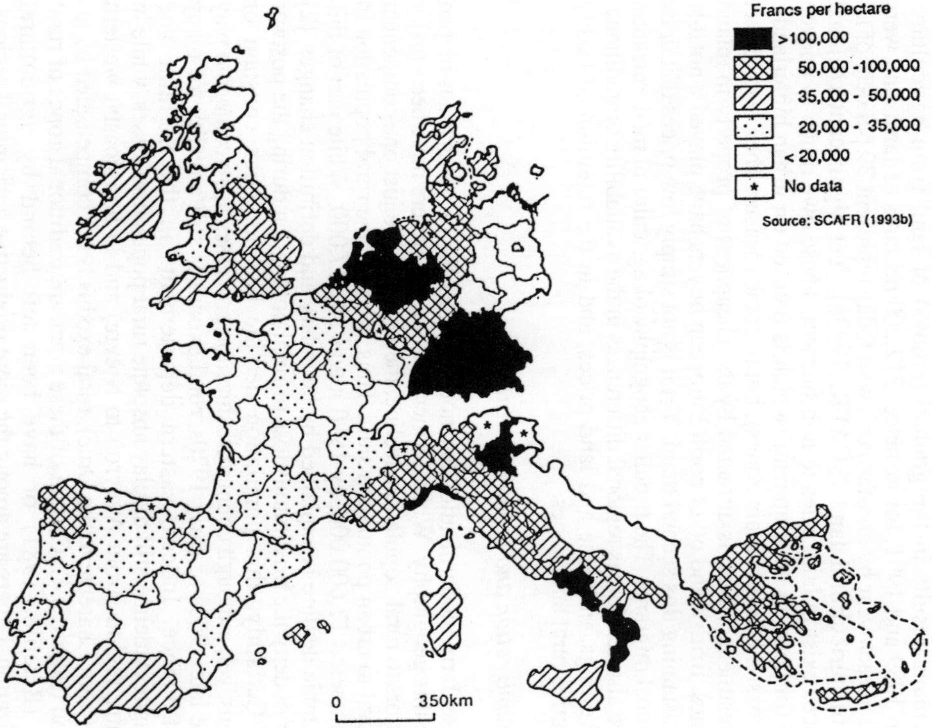

Francs per hectare

■	>100,000
▨	50,000 -100,000
▧	35,000 - 50,000
⋮	20,000 - 35,000
☐	< 20,000
✳	No data

Source: SCAFR (1993b)

0   350km

Figure 2.3   Agricultural land prices in the EC

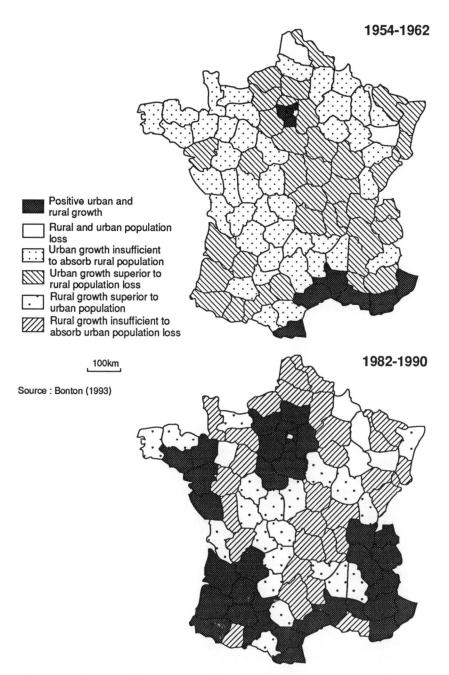

1954-1962

Positive urban and
rural growth

Rural and urban population
loss

Urban growth insufficient
to absorb rural population

Urban growth superior to
rural population loss

Rural growth superior to
urban population

Rural growth insufficient to
absorb urban population loss

100km

Source : Bonton (1993)

1982-1990

Figure 2.4   **Urban and rural population change, 1954-1962 and
1982-1990**

21

Table 2.2   **Annual percentage population change in rural France by size of commune, 1954-1982**

Commune population	1954-1962	1962-1968	1968-1975	1975-1982
Under 50	-2.54	-2.24	-2.39	-2.25
50 - 90	-1.59	-1.79	-1.90	-0.97
100 - 199	-1.06	-1.39	-1.45	-0.31
200 - 499	-0.66	-0.92	-0.84	0.36
500 - 999	-0.24	-0.38	-0.06	0.99
1 000 - 1 999	0.21	1.17	0.68	-1.34
2 000 and over	0.53	0.42	1.08	1.67
All rural areas	-0.45	-0.44	-0.12	0.06

Source: INSEE (1954, 1962, 1968, 1975, 1982) *Recensement Généraux de la Population*, Paris

pattern still persists today is confirmed by the 1990 Census, which showed that rural communes with less than 200 inhabitants had fewer intercensal in-migrants than more populated rural communes (with a mean average of 28.0 per cent of the commune population, compared with 32.0 per cent; see INSEE, 1991b).

The years between 1950 and the early 1970s were particularly important for rural France, as this was the apogee of the longstanding trend of rural migration losses. During this period population was lost not simply in relative terms but also in absolute numbers, with the role of rural areas as foyers for the French population declining irrevocably. For the first time in France's history, the town became the dominant residential location for French people. Yet, consistent with trends in much of Europe (Fielding, 1982), as we move further into the 1970s we see the build up of counterurbanization forces that have brought migrants back to rural France. Even so, the French counterurbanization experience has been neither as intense nor as general as its British counterpart.

Patterns of counterurbanization

The principal direction of French internal migration has been clear throughout the twentieth century. The main destinations of those leaving rural areas were initially the major regional cities, notably Lyon, Marseille and the Paris agglomeration; all of which experienced explosive and often unplanned growth (Scargill, 1983). In more recent decades, declining growth in the major cities has been matched by population increases in lower order urban centres (of up to 20,000 inhabitants). These towns continue to register population gains, but rural areas, although most evidently when close to larger urban centres, have since overtaken them (Laborie, 1993). Even so, rural demographic revival has been equivocal. Indeed, while studies have highlighted counterurbanization processes in many countries (Vining and Pallone, 1982; Champion, 1989), in an international context the notion of a new counterurbanization trend in France raises some difficulty in identifying a 'clean break' with past migration trends. Effectively, metropolitan decentralization is not easily distinguished from genuine demographic deconcentration (Buller, 1991).

To appreciate the issues involved here, it is pertinent to highlight the main phases of postwar internal migration. The first phase, which stretched from 1954 to 1968, was one of unequivocal rural to urban migration, with rural areas experiencing absolute population decline. A second phase, which covered the intercensal period 1968-1975, showed early signs of a reversal in the fortunes of rural areas; although an important distinction has to be drawn between areas close to larger urban centres and more peripheral locations. Moreover, during this second phase, rural areas as a whole experienced net outmigration. Only in the third period, from 1975-1990, did the majority of rural French communes register a positive migration balance (for the first time in 150 years), although some rural zones continued to display net population decline (Table 2.3). As in Britain, the counterurbanization literature in France identifies a broad range of economic and social factors that account for a shift in residential choices in favour of the countryside. Thus, the desire for a better lifestyle or for improved housing has been shown to dominate the migration decisions of newcomers to the Languedoc uplands (Catanzano, 1987), as well as those who 'escaped' Grenoble (David et al., 1980). This is not to say that economic considerations are not significant. However, there is inconsistency over their impact. Some studies report that economic necessity is significantly absent as a motivation for changing homes (Kayser, 1989, p.59), even though rural population growth is associated with the deconcentration of economic activities from urban centres (Muller et al., 1989; Bontron, 1993). Perhaps this confusion is not so different from Britain, where longer distance commuting, job relocations, retirement migration and more socially motivated residential changes all seem to be part of the rural population turnaround (Jones et al., 1986; Bolton and Chalkley, 1990; Cross, 1990).

However, the French counterurbanization experience does differ from that of Britain in that it is largely limited to periurban zones and is accompanied by a persistent rural exodus from more distant rural regions (Noin, 1984; Buller, 1991). It follows that a crucial factor in understanding migration from urban to rural France is the concept of industrial and urban hinterlands. In France these are formalized into a distinct territorial category, the *Zones de Peuplement Industriel ou Urbain* (ZPIU). These areas are defined and revised by the national statistical agency according to an ensemble of social and economic criteria that include place of work, the proportion of farmers amongst the active population and the presence of newly installed industrial and commercial enterprises. [3] For our purposes, the significance of the ZPIU designation is that it identifies rural areas that

Table 2.3   **French population change by settlement type, 1975-1990**

	1975	1982	1990	% change 1975-1990
France	52 656	54 335	56 614	6.9
Urban centres	23 565	23 413	23 540	-0.1
Suburbs	15 455	16 446	17 597	12.1
Rural areas within ZPIU	7 827	8 746	9 687	19.2
Rural areas outside ZPIU	5 809	5 731	5 791	-0.3

Source: INSEE (1975, 1982, 1990) *Recensement Généraux de la Population,* Paris

are closely tied to nearby urban centres. It thus creates a fundamental distinction between rural communes that are 'urban oriented' and those that lie outside an urban hinterland (commonly known as the 'profoundly rural' communes). As Table 2.3 shows, rural migration patterns within and beyond ZPIU are substantially different, as are their occupational compositions (INSEE, 1988). Since 1975 rural communes within a ZPIU have exhibited the fastest growth rates of all French communes, whether rural or urban (Faur, 1991). Profoundly rural communes have not only been late to register positive demographic changes (essentially only after the 1982 census and even that failed to bring this group of communes back to their 1975 population levels; see Table 2.3), but what changes have been experienced have been slight compared with other communes. Rural communes therefore fall into both the fastest and the slowest growing units of demographic change. This calls into question both the pertinence of an all embracing concept of rural (Hoggart, 1990) and the genuineness of counterurbanization as a process of broad rural revitalization in France (Buller, 1991). Indeed, given the centrifugal nature of French rural to urban migration, it is perhaps more accurate to refer to it as 'rurbanization' (Berger and Fruit, 1980), as it largely involves low density peripheral urban expansion (Bauer and Roux, 1976). The critical point to emphasize is that rural to urban migration in France is predominantly a process of urban deconcentration, with ex-urban migrants revealing a distinctly 'suburban' propensity to occupy new, purpose built rural homes rather than older, more traditionally styled rural dwellings (Belliard and Boyer, 1983). Given this tendency, plus the fact that the highest rates of new house building in rural and small town France are in the mountain areas of the southeast and in coastal départements, with low rates being notable in western départements (Troufleau, 1992), it is not difficult to infer that western départements are attracting comparatively few French ex-urbanites. Most certainly, inflows are too small to have a significant bearing on the number of vacant homes in peripheral rural communes.

The complexity of the rural population turnaround in France has prompted calls for a move away from strict numerical assessments of population movement toward more anthropological examinations of migrant decisions (Courgeau and Lelievre, 1989); a demand that finds echoes in Vartiainen's (1989) critique of counterurbanization models as a whole. The relative proximity of the rural experience for a large part of the French urban and periurban population complicates Anglo-Saxon models of urban flight and rural discovery. Over the last 150 years, British society has reinvented 'the countryside' in a manner that matches its own cultural mores more than the reality of rural living (Williams, 1973; Keith, 1974). Moreover, having developed so idealized an image of rurality, increasing numbers of city dwellers have sought to locate themselves in the countryside. French urban society, by contrast, is both younger and less removed from its rural antecedents, and appears less inclined to romanticize the countryside. Certainly, at this point in time, there is no rush out of the cities toward more distant places. Only second home and retirement migration reveal aspects of this, with the dominant trend in rural in-migration being firmly tied to proximate urban centres.

Retirement migration and second home ownership

The migration of British nationals to rural France needs to be interpreted not only in the context of general migration trends, but also in terms of moves that are not employment related; whether these be linked to retirement (Warnes, 1991a) or tourism (Valenzuela, 1993). Such considerations are particularly pertinent because the 'deeply rural' focus of many of British moves potentially points to a unique contribution of British citizens to French migration patterns. However, before such an assumption can be assessed, both retirement migration and second home purchases within France need to be examined. Both have shown a tendency to be drawn toward more peripheral rural locales.

Retirement migration By 1990, retired households were the largest single household group in rural France (Table 2.4), representing some 40 per cent of all households. [4] In terms of their distribution, a key distinction must again be drawn between rural communes within a defined urban hinterland (ZPIU), where retired households constituted 33.7 per cent of the total, and those lying beyond, where they represented 43.0 per cent (INSEE, 1991a, pp.148-153). Figures for urban areas fall well below these, at 27.4 per cent. Moreover, as Table 2.4 demonstrates, not only is the number of retired people growing (from 13.6 per cent of the French population in 1982, to 16.2 per cent in 1992), but so too is the relative importance of the rural retired population. In part, this is explained by the demographic evolution of the indigenous rural population (Paillat, 1986). In particular, outmigration by younger people and the ageing of the remaining population has resulted in a substantial retired population in more peripheral places. Yet this has been added to by retirement into rural areas. Indeed, as Cribier (1979) has amply demonstrated urban to rural moves represent a dominant trend in French

Table 2.4   **Percentage occupational composition of rural households in France, 1962-1990**

Occupation	1962	1990
Agriculture	33.8	9.9
Artisans - commerce	8.8	6.9
White collar	3.9	14.9
Employees and manual workers	25.0	27.6
Retired farmers	7.1	11.1
Other retired	21.4	29.6

Source: Bontron (1993)

retirement migration. Thus, in a study of retirement migrants from Paris, Cribier revealed that 49.6 per cent relocated to rural communes, with a further 16 per cent moving to small towns of under 10,000 inhabitants in rural regions (thus, making the total for 'rural regions' some 65 per cent; Cribier, 1993). Amongst those who had selected a rural commune, 44 per cent had moved to a 'profoundly rural' area. In an earlier survey, a similar Parisian propensity for rural locations was identified, with 27 per cent of retirees relocating to a hamlet or isolated dwelling and a further 26 per cent moving to an old village centre (Cribier, 1982, p.127).

Motivations for retirement migration in Anglo-Saxon countries fall into a number of broad, seemingly universal categories: first, the desire to locate in specific 'retirement regions', which are frequently chosen for their amenity value, as with coastal resorts (Karn, 1977); secondly, the attraction of areas of prior family connections (Warnes, 1986; Longino, 1992); and, thirdly, the rediscovery of a region of origin. A distinctive feature of French retirement migration is the importance of this third motivation (Cribier, 1980); which, on account of relatively the late urbanization of France, results in contemporary flows from urban to rural areas. Thus, a third of the Parisian retirement migrants analyzed by Cribier (1982) specifically retired to the *pays* in which they or their partner was born; although this meant returning to a general region rather than to a specific village for the majority. Taken alone, this would suggest that patterns of retirement migration are as dispersed as the origins of city in-migrants. However, an important element in the geography of French retirement migration has been the 'unequal ability' of regions to draw back those who previous left them (Cribier, 1993, p.10). The Paris Basin exerts the most effective pull on its emigres, followed by Brittany, the Mediterranean coast, the Pyrénées and the south west, while the north and north east and the Massif Central emerge with the weakest return migrant flows. Significantly, the former group are also the most attractive regions for those retired migrants who have no specific connections with them.

With every new generation, French society becomes more distant from its rural antecedents. As fewer urban dwellers claim direct rural origins, a decline in retirement migration to areas of prior residence is to be expected. This does appear to be occurring, as rural locales are now being selected for reasons other than the search for past origins (Cribier, 1993). Moreover, proximity to family does not offer an effective explanation for the growing number of moves to rural areas. This is because the majority of retired migrants place a greater distance between themselves and their kin by their move (Cribier, 1982). With rural retirement destinations now being more common amongst born and bred Parisians than amongst prior in-migrants to Paris, the supposition that amenity and quality of life considerations are increasingly important in retirement decisions gains force (Cribier, 1993). Indeed, according to Cribier (1993, p.12), a comparison of the geography of current retirement migration with holiday destinations in the 1960s shows a 'startling resemblance'. Yet, while retirement migration in France might be losing some of its international distinctiveness, in favour of a more common dispersed pattern that accompanies the search for amenity rich environments (Warnes, 1991a), at this point retirement flows are still dominated by specific destinations. Hence, irrespective of whether the countryside has failed to offer a viable milieu during economically productive years, it does have attractions as a consumption site for retirement. Yet it is still true that remoter rural regions are weaker magnets for retirees than more coastal or otherwise tourist oriented areas.

Second home ownership The second home phenomenon is a longstanding one in France. Strong family links between rural and urban areas, plus the stipulations of French inheritance laws (Cribier, 1973; Clout, 1977), combine to make rates of rural second home ownership among the highest in Europe (Lenfant and Seyer, 1980). Within France, second homes have long interested researchers; owing to their impact on seasonal migration (Thomas, 1977), their effect on rural property markets (Dourlens and Vidal-Naquet, 1980), their implications for host communities (Bonnain and Sautter, 1970; Mirloup, 1977) and their role in rural regeneration (Kalaora and Brun, 1985). The 1990 census identified 2,814,291 second homes in metropolitan France (against an estimated 200,000 in Britain; Shucksmith, 1983). This represents a 24.2 per cent growth since 1982 (INSEE, 1991a), which can be compared with a 9.9 per cent growth in the number of principal homes over the same period. Currently, second homes represent around 10.7 per cent of the total housing stock (Table 2.5). As one would expect, regional variation exists both in their absolute number and in their share of the total housing stock (Figure 2.5). Their highest incidence is found in the Provençal départements of Var, Alpes Maritimes and Hérault (which together account for 13 per cent of all French second homes), followed by the alpine départements of Savoie and Haute Savoie, by Brittany and by the greater Paris region. The Paris region is important here not simply because of the incidence of weekend homes in départements around the city but also as a result of of pied-à-terre apartments within the city. Like Provence, the Alpes and Brittany, the Paris Basin is as much of a second

Table 2.5   Changing housing types in France, 1975-1990

	1975		1982		1990	
	Number (000s)	%	Number (000s)	%	Number (000s)	%
First homes	17 729	84.2	19 588	82.6	21 535	82.0
Second homes	1 693	8.0	2 265	9.5	2 814	10.7
Vacant homes	1 607	7.8	1 854	7.9	1 895	7.3
Total	21 029	100.0	23 707	100.0	26 245	100.0

Source: INSEE (1975, 1982, 1990) *Recensement Généraux de la Population*, Paris

home location today as it was 25 years ago (Brier, 1970). As such, these geographical foci illustrate two of principal motives in second home location; proximity to a first home and amenity value.

What should be noted is that years of rural depopulation and a resulting abundance of cheap rural housing have meant that neither house prices nor housing availability have imposed much constraint on second home ownership (Cribier, 1973). Without doubt, higher income groups dominate second home possession (Kalaora and Brun, 1985). Nonetheless, second home owning is by not negligible amongst other socio-economic groups; as indicated by Kayser's (1989, p.174) suggestion that around 6.5 per cent of blue collar families possess a second home (albeit the figure is 28 per cent for company owners, managers and professionals). In the past, a major reason for this was the Napoleonic system of inheritance, which ensures an equal division of parental goods amongst all direct offspring. Thus, a number of ex-rural families can find themselves the joint or single owner of homes that once belonged to their parents. Illustrative of this effect, in a study of the Breton département of the Côtes d'Armor, Kalaora and Brun (1985, p.24) cite a 48.7 per cent rate for second home acquisition through inheritance, against 48.9 per cent that were obtained by purchase (see also Cribier, 1973). However, with fewer urbanites as first generation migrants, we can expect inheritance to play a lesser part in second home acquisition; with the likely consequence that the geographical pattern of linkages that bind first and second homes will change in the future.

Inheritance is not the sole factor that needs to be considered. Thus, in a study that Kalaora and Brun (1985) cite, we learn that the majority of owners in a rural study département were born in the commune in which they bought or inherited their second home. It was only amongst second home owners who built their own home that non-natives dominated (Bonneau, 1978). However, purpose built dwellings are much more

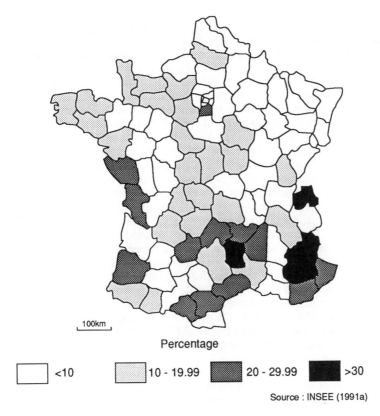

Percentage

<10   10 - 19.99   20 - 29.99   >30

Source : INSEE (1991a)

**Figure 2.5   Second homes in 1990 as a percentage of the housing
            stock, by département**

common in coastal and alpine locations, with newly built homes being under
represented in the remoter areas of départements in western France. Yet rural
areas still have an important second home representation. Thus, whereas
second homes comprised 10.7 per cent of all French housing in 1990,
virtually all rural départements in southern and western France record higher
figures, with the range including 45.8 per cent in the Alpes, 26 per cent in
the Pyrénéen département of Ariège, 20.7 per cent in Charente Maritime and
19.5 per cent in Calvados (Figure 2.5). Moreover, while second homes are
numerous in urban centres (Kalaora and Brun, 1985), of the 2.26 million
second homes recorded in the 1982 census, around 1.3 million were in rural
areas, with 700,000 in profoundly rural communes (INSEE, 1984)

Even so, coastal and mountain regions dominate the map of second home
owning; much as they did in the late 1960s (Leroux, 1968). Here we should
note that the link between vacant rural dwellings and second home
ownership is not strong. Were this the case, remoter rural regions would see

more second home acquisitions by French citizens who have weak local ties. This does not seem to be happening (Kalaora and Brun, 1985). And if vacant properties were a primary attraction, then rates of second home ownership should be inversely related to vacant housing numbers. In a few départements this is the case. In Dordogne, for instance, a 36.2 per cent growth in second homes between 1982 and 1990 was accompanied by a 6.7 per cent fall in the number of vacant houses, while in Haute Savoie the figures were 50 per cent and 25 per cent, respectively. However, in other regions, most notably in Corsica and the Pyrénées, both second homes and vacant housing are increasing. Elsewhere, in coastal and mountain départements, notably in Provence, the Landes and the north west, much second home accommodation is both purpose built and urban (Bontron, 1989). Here, vacant housing draws few new home buyers. Only in rural départements of southern and western France does there appear to be a clear relationship between rates of second home growth and vacant housing decline. However, even this represents only a limited rediscovery of rural life, for relatively small numbers are being attracted by rural landscapes and an idealized rural pace of life, rather than by water or mountains. For some commentators, the restricted appeal of second home ownership in what Britons would regard as the 'traditional countryside' is indicative of a growing social exclusivity of this housing form; which distinguishes it from the broader social base of coastal apartment ownership (Marié and Viard, 1977). Indeed, if more second homes are to be acquired because of their specifically rural location, then this could form the basis for a fundamental geographical and social cleavage between second homes as short term accessible consumption items and second homes as an affirmation of a longer term lifestyle choice. The strength of British home purchases in remoter parts of rural France perhaps indicates that one of the vanguards for such a change could come from across the Channel.

The revalorization of French rural space

Current trends in internal migration point to a sea change in the role and function of rural France; which Kayser has termed 'renaissance' (1989) or 'birth' (1993). At one level, this change has been founded upon a rejection of the speed and style of postwar urbanization. Thus, the *maison individuelle* at the urban periphery is replacing the centre city *apartement*, while *parcs d'haute technologie* in regional cities become new foci for industrial growth. These are familiar changes for the Anglo-Saxon reader. Their individuality in the French case lies largely in their late appearance, plus the fact that they have come so close on the heels of centralization and urbanization. Yet, at another level, these trends point to a major, if subtle, reinvention of the countryside as a residential consumption site, rather than as a productive environment (Barbichon, 1973). Compared with Britain, this reinvention has been sudden and dramatic. As a consequence it has been surrounded by considerable economic, political and social tension; as revealed in the clear separation of votes in the Maastricht referendum between rural and urban France, and between areas of peasant and modern farm structures. Certainly, the diversification of rural France is largely a feature of residential change, rather than of occupational opportunity. Manufacturing employment remains essentially urban based, while the growing number of blue collar workers in the countryside arguably results more from improved commuting links than any genuine industrial relocation. For remoter rural areas, the key growth sectors are still tied to the maintenance and improvement of a residential environment and to vacation opportunities (Béteille, 1992).

For Britons seeking to invest in a permanent or a second home in France, the changes that the French countryside has undergone since 1945 have undoubtedly made it more available to outside buyers. Perhaps the increased interest that French citizens are now showing in living in their countryside enhances the potential for direct competition between British and French buyers. However, with French interest focused largely on rural zones close to urban centres and with much of the remainder of rural France still registering demographic and economic decline, British and French buyers commonly have their eyes set on different geographical fields. In Britain, the wealthier and more mobile middle classes, who are more able to afford and take advantage of a rural residence, find the imagery of living in the countryside particularly attractive (Thrift, 1989; Crouch, 1992). Moreover, as various studies indicate, the appeal of rural living finds significant expression in remoter rural areas (Forsythe, 1980; Jones et al., 1986; Bolton and Chalkley, 1990; Phillips, 1993), with the geography of rural in-migration in Britain changing over time as new areas are sought out or gain popularity (Cross, 1990). Yet a consequence of this population shift has been a reduced sense of rurality. Not only is the British countryside threatened by growing investment by house builders (Elson, 1986; Hoggart, 1993) but rural life is itself succumbing to more 'urbanized' cultural, economic and social trends which threaten 'idealized' images of rurality. Evidence from British Social Attitude surveys, for instance, indicates that there is widespread recognition that the British countryside is changing; with most evaluating these changes negatively (Young, 1988).

Of course, change in the British countryside is not uniform. As a consequence, we might expect dissimilar intensities of 'disappointment' with countryside change. Most certainly, when we examine our household survey evidence to see if British home buyers in France come from different parts of their home nation, we see clear inter-regional differences. Thus, of the 406 British property owners we interviewed in five French départements, South East England (with or without London) stands out as the dominant place of origin for British buyers (Table 2.6). To our knowledge, there has been no systematic survey of regional attitudes on how wholesome or 'safe' the British countryside is felt to be. Although anecdotal comments suggest that people in the South East must go outside their region for any 'genuine' rurality; as in Fielding's (1992) assertion that the South East is less 'place full' and more banal than other parts of Britain. But while such sentiments might jell with popular sentiments, they require a more solid empirical foundation before we can be comfortable with the idea that this is central cause of home buying in 'truly rural' France. Certainly, there is merit in Fielding's (1992) notion that the South East is more akin to a non-place urban realm than other parts of Britain; for the greater population density,

Table 2.6   British home regions of French property buyers

	% with first home now in France	% with a second home in France	Purchase rate per million people, 1991
Britain			
South East, except London	28.4	43.0	12.9
London	15.3	19.3	10.0
South West	17.4	8.7	10.6
West Midlands	2.7	5.8	3.2
Yorkshire and Humberside	3.3	3.9	2.8
North West	3.3	3.4	2.0
East Anglia	3.8	1.9	5.3
Wales	2.2	2.9	3.5
East Midlands	2.7	2.4	2.5
North	2.7	1.4	2.6
Scotland	1.1	1.0	0.8
Northern Ireland	0.0	0.0	0.0
Elsewhere			
France	4.4	1.5	-
Other Europe	5.5	3.9	-
Africa	3.3	0.0	-
Australasia	1.6	0.0	-
The Americas	0.5	1.5	-
Asia	0.5	0.0	-

Source: Authors' survey

higher incidence of job changes and growing influence of London on the character and distribution of population in this region (Warnes, 1991b), all militate in this direction. Middle class opposition to further housing growth in the South East also points to an underlying disquiet over landscape change in the region (Short et al., 1986). But even if British landscape differences are not a key causal force, comparisons between South East England and remoter rural areas in France certainly offer a stark contrast. In part, this is because France as a whole retains more of a 'rural culture' than Britain. But its more rural areas enhance this sense by offering a distinctiveness from urban centres that is expressed in both landscape and social terms (particularly in the south and west). At the same time, as a consequence of rural depopulation, agricultural modernization and a French disposition toward newly built properties, rural France offers an abundance of traditionally styled dwellings for sale. This stands in marked contrast with the availability of property in the British countryside (Shucksmith, 1990).

Yet this contrast arises not simply because of the type of property that is available, but also due to its relative price.

Property price differentials

To understand linkages between migrant origins and destinations, it is not sufficient to focus solely on the conditions of receiving areas (Mabogunje, 1970). Also to be taken into account is the character, and processes of change that impinge on that character, of migrant origins. This applies irrespective of whether we are concerned with those who permanently relocate their home or those who engage in seasonal migration. In addition, irrespective of whether migration is conceptualized as 'push', 'pull' or a combination of the two, we need to understand how potential migrants identify and satisfy themselves about the character of alternative destinations. For the purposes of this book, it is not our intention to go into detail about this, but it is appropriate to indicate that a primary mechanism through which British citizens became aware of the possibilities and attractions of French home owning was through the activities of a small number of British companies that publicized French property sales (Hoggart and Buller, 1992a). This activity gained potency because it popularized French property ownership, both through direct advertising and, more influentially, through feeding articles and information to the press for more general coverage (Hoggart and Buller, 1994a). As the owner of one of the earliest British companies in this property market reported to us, after 'many, many years of cultivation' efforts to promote French property sales began to pay off when 'the literate found it the fashionable thing to do' and it became the 'talk of the cocktail set'. The impact this had is demonstrated in reports by those who eventually became French home owners:

> There comes a time when you stop looking in French estate agents' windows to see the kind of thing other people have been buying and decide to join the second home owners club (France) yourself. (Barnes, 1991)

But while such sentiments strengthened French property sales in Britain, they were not sufficient to stimulate the volume that occurred in the late 1980s. Had this been the case, then the rapid acceleration of sales would not have taken so many British and French property firms by surprise (Hoggart and Buller, 1992a; Buller and Hoggart, 1993). In fact, the majority of companies that promote French property sales in Britain entered this market only after sales had expanded significantly. Given this, it is clear that we need to look beyond property companies if we are to explain why British property ownership in France increased so rapidly during 1988.

A realistic explanation for the boom in British home acquisitions between 1988 and 1990 was the rapid rise in house prices in Britain. This not only helps account for the dominance of buyers from South East England (Table 2.6), but also explains the timing of increased demand for a French home. It is not simply that housing is more expensive in the South East, but also that cheaper rural housing, even that in need of major repairs, is in

Table 2.7   Percentage gain in UK house prices, 1983-1988

Region	% change	Region	% change
Outer Metropolitan	128.8	East Anglia	123.1
Outer South East	120.2	Wales	42.2
Greater London	140.8	East Midlands	66.3
South West	96.2	North	35.3
West Midlands	62.4	Scotland	30.3
Yorkshire & Humberside	43.7	Northern Ireland	18.6
North West	43.6	UK	71.4

Source: Nationwide Anglia Building Society (1993) *House Prices in 1993: Third Quarter of 1993*, London

shorter supply in this region than elsewhere in Britain (Department of the Environment, 1988). In addition, just before the 1988 acceleration in British home acquisitions in France, house prices in the South East were rising faster than anywhere in country (Table 2.7, using equivalent regions to Table 2.6). With the notable exception of East Anglia (where elderly in-migration has affected local housing markets for some time, and most likely continues to do so, given the recent disproportionate rise in the elderly population of this region; Warnes and Ford, 1993) and, to a lesser extent, the East Midlands, there is a close direct relationship between house price rises between 1983-1988 and the home locations of our sample of British home owners in France (and the East Anglia anomaly disappears if purchase levels are standardized by the population of each region).

That house prices were a critical economic, political and social issue in Britain at this time, and particularly in the South East, is readily seen in the problems created by housing affordability (e.g. Barlow and Savage, 1991). In this context, advertising about French property must have drawn attention to the feasibility of home owning over the Channel. This follows because even a cursory glance at newspaper and magazine articles focuses the attention of any reader on the comparatively low price of French homes. Thus, even if we take the first quarter of 1992, when mean average house prices were 28.7 per cent lower than in the same quarter of 1989 in the Outer South East, 26.2 per cent lower in the Outer Metropolitan Area and 25.8 per cent lower in Greater London, the mean average price for a detached house in these regions was £100,710, £135,413 and £159,676, respectively. By contrast, at the same time, it was being reported that in Mayenne: 'For £15,000 buyers get a nice little village house; for £25,000, they can have a farmhouse with barns and outbuildings within half an hour's drive of the coast' (Gates, 1992a). Likewise, in Brittany: 'It is still possible to buy a run down old fermette for about £8,000, but it will be just a shell ...'

Table 2.8   **Prices paid for a property with a dwelling by British buyers in the arrondissement of Sarlat, Dordogne, 1988-1992**

	£30 000 or less	£30 001-£60 000	£60 001-£100 000	£100 001-£200 000	More than £200 000
Number of buyers	37	59	16	32	12
Percentage of buyers	23.7	37.8	10.3	20.5	7.7

Source: Own compilation from SAFER, *Notifications d'Acte de Vente*, Périgord

(Russell, 1991b). Southern locations also had cheap offerings, as in '... Languedoc Roussillon, where properties to restore can be snapped up for around £10,000 ...' (Elliott, 1992). That low prices are to be expected throughout France is suggested by the cost of agricultural land (Figure 2.3) and the extent of housing abandonment in rural areas (Figure 2.1). That most British buyers have been able to acquire French homes cheaply is further shown by examining SAFER land transaction records. Thus, even for the relatively high priced département of Dordogne (Buller and Hoggart, 1993), the norm has been for Britons to pay significantly less for a home than would be expected in Britain (Table 2.8). Indicative of this, during the boom 1988-1990 years, the average price paid by foreign buyers in Brittany (around 90 per cent of which were reported to be British) was 185,000 Francs (or about £18,500 at the 1989 exchange rate; see Cellule Economique de Bretagne, 1990, p.90).

Media coverage did have a role to play here, not simply in drawing attention to the prices of French homes but also in emphasizing the ready availability of such properties. Where the reality of British housing markets intersected with this information, and so created a dramatic increase in British house buying, was not simply in the fact that house prices were rising rapidly in the UK, but also because of the ready availability of credit for house purchases. Here, the substantial wealth that is invested in British homes has a critical part to play, for both British and French banks (and British building societies) were more than happy to make loans using the value of an existing home as security (Hamnett, 1992). However, it is also the case that with low prices in France, many buyers were able to pay for their property with cash; with a readership survey by the magazine *French Property News* finding that 61.3 per cent of existing owners used cash to buy their French home (Wisefile Ltd, 1992). For second home owners, the source of cash payments came from savings, insurance policy maturities or inheritance receipts (e.g. Hamnett et al., 1989). Here the impact of rising British house prices would be indirect, in that it provoked media attention

Table 2.9   **Percentage of British households with members in various occupational categories**

Occupation of at least one adult in a household	Household with no retired members		Retired households +
	First home owners	Second home owners	
Artists	12.6	6.2	7.7
Company directors	11.6	22.8	22.2
Farmers	11.6	0.0	4.3
Lecturers *	5.3	8.0	6.0
Managers	6.3	11.1	20.5
Manual workers	16.8	3.7	2.6
Professions ^	1.1	9.3	4.3
Teachers	23.2	22.8	18.8

Notes:

+   This refers to households comprised of persons of retirement age alone or a retired person and her or his partner. The former constitutes 82.4 per cent of 'retired' households. The table does not include households which were less easily located on a retired - non-retired divide (as with retired parents living with their adult children). No other occupational category was recorded for more than 15 households.

*   This includes university and further education lecturers, as responses do not allow us to distinguish between them in all mail questionnaires.

^   Computed for those professions with 'chartered' qualifications (such as accountants, solicitors and surveyors)

Source: Authors' survey

on the cheapness of French property (as well as the enticing 'unspoilt' rural landscapes in which properties were located). For those who relied on a mortgage or who changed their main home, property prices had a more direct impact. Here, the ability to sell a home in Britain at an inflated price (owing to sharp house price increases), or to use the value of a home as collateral on a further mortgage, provided a substantial capital stock from which to buy a French home and, for first home buyers, surplus funds on which to draw an income or start a new enterprise (e.g. from interest payments or from establishing an enterprise with the capital).

Conclusion

Critical to understanding British migration to rural France is an appreciation of the underlying appeal of 'the countryside' to the British middle classes (e.g. Williams, 1973), for they comprise the overwhelming majority of British buyers (Table 2.9). Adding to this underlying appeal, in recent years the consumption of 'symbols' like rurality has grown in importance in Britain relative to the consumption of products for their use value (Lash and Urry, 1987; Thrift, 1989; Crouch, 1992). It is no surprising, then, that late 1980s advertising made French home owning 'the talk of the cocktail set'. Its appeal was aided by a characteristic British appreciation of the investment value and potential future returns from home ownership (Forrest and Murie, 1990). Given the boom in British house prices and the cheapness of French property, this appreciation no doubt enhanced the attractions of cross Channel purchases (especially when permanent home changes were sought). Yet the cheapness of French homes was merely one manifestation of processes than have dominated remoter rural areas in this nation for some decades. In the form of rural depopulation, agricultural modernization and few alternatives to farm employment, these created a surplus of old and traditionally built properties of low cost; this cheapness arising not simply because of the number of available properties but also because there was little demand for them within the internal housing market. As such, rural France offered British buyers an accessible, 'truly rural' environment that was either unattainable or too expensive to acquire in Britain.

Notes

1   Vacant houses are defined by the government statistical office as housing available for sale or rent, housing built but awaiting either sale or occupation and additional dwellings other than second homes which were unoccupied at the time of the census.
2   The formal definition of a rural commune has altered significantly over the years. The longstanding definition of an urban commune is a commune that exceeds a population of 2,000 residents who live in a built up area (rural communes do not exceed this threshold). However, this has been modified by changes to the definition of a 'built up' area. Immediately following the Second World War, this was defined as dwellings separated by less than 50 metres. It has subsequently become 200 metres, which has allowed a far greater number of houses to be included in built areas. This has had the effect of redefining some communes as urban even though they have experienced no gain in population.
3   Initially defined at the time of the 1962 population census, the *Zones de Peuplement Industriel ou Urbain* (ZPIU) are composed of urban and

rural communes; typically one or a number of urban centres plus their surrounding rural communes that have an 'industrial' or 'dormitory' function. These units are assessed by reference to commuting patterns, the proportion of the population that works locally, the percentage of the workforce that are farmers, the number of industrial units and so on.

4   The French census classes socio-economic groups into eight specific 'socio-professional' categories. One of these is 'retired people', which is defined as those people living on a retirement pension. The statistics presented here concern this socio-professional category in terms of rural households, where socio-professional standing is defined by the occupation of the head of household.

3 The British as an immigrant group in France

France has long cherished its international role as a sanctuary for political refugees (Limousin, 1988) and a *pays d'acceuil* for foreign nationals (Le Bras and Todd, 1981). Although both are today the subject of much internal soul searching, recent Europe-wide opinion polls demonstrate that a vast number of non-French nationals regard France as a highly desired place to live and work (e.g. Renucci, 1990). This long standing popularity owes much to the relative economic health and political stability of France; both of which have helped draw Italian and Spanish immigrants in the past and are current attractions for would be migrants from northern and central Africa; with many such immigrants coming from states that were former colonies or protectorates of France. In addition, France has offered intellectual, cultural and lifestyle attractions that have drawn the privileged of Europe and the world throughout this and the last century. In more recent years, France has come to be appreciated equally for its space, the physical beauty of its environment and the quality of life that is enjoyed by its residents. Yet the character of immigrant flows into France is not uniform. While British migrants are attracted by the French countryside, this certainly does not apply for most immigrants, nor even for other inflows from northern Europe. This means that there are different geographies to foreign nationals within France. In so far as immigrant moves have associated economic, political and social implications, this points to British in-migration having different consequences from that of other groups. To appreciate this distinction, this chapter seeks to establish the peculiar character of British migrants in terms of general trends in French immigration.

International migration to France

Our intention here is not to present a history of international migration to France, for there is a considerable literature on this subject already, both in English and in French (e.g. George, 1986a; Ogden, 1989; Amar and Milza, 1990). But it is pertinent to stress that the British are a small component of

39

Table 3.1   The evolution of the foreign population in France, 1921-1990

Year	Foreigners (000s)	Foreigners as % of total population
1921	1 532	3.95
1926	2 409	5.99
1931	2 715	6.58
1936	2 198	5.34
1946	1 744	4.38
1954	1 765	4.12
1962	2 170	4.67
1968	2 621	5.28
1975	3 442	6.54
1982	3 714	6.84
1990	3 597	6.35

Source: Derived from INSEE (1992)

the immigrant population in France, and that their presence in significant numbers is quite recent. These two points are not unconnected, as the long history of immigration into France has given that nation a substantial population of resident 'foreigners'. Thus, of a 1991 population of 56,561,955, some 3,596,602 French residents were foreign nationals (6.3 per cent). This absolute figure is less than that recorded at the 1982 census, when the foreign population was at its maximum, and the relative standing of foreign residents is now slightly smaller than it was in each of 1982 (6.8 per cent), 1975 (6.5 per cent) and even 1931 (see Table 3.1). But despite significant losses through return migration (e.g. Cazorla Pérez, 1989; King and Rybaczuk, 1993) and naturalization (e.g. Boisvert, 1987), there has been a continuing inflow of foreign citizens into France since the Second World War. This movement was relatively slow up to the mid 1950s but there was precipitous growth from then until the late 1970s, with another period of lesser growth in recent years. The 1960s certainly represents the third great wave of immigration into France (Noin, 1991), with the first and second waves occurring in the late nineteenth century and the interwar years. This third wave has been closely linked to the industrial and urban transformation of France since 1945 (Levy and Garson, 1991), to the break up of the French colonial empire (Mottin, 1992) and to the enactment of specific agreements between France and other nations (notably Italy). In the 1960s, the foreign population grew rapidly at 2-3 per cent per annum. More recently, with the onset of economic downturn and the introduction of more restrictive immigration policies by successive French governments (Papademetriou, 1988; Weil, 1988), growth has become virtually negligible

Table 3.2   **Percentage of all foreign nationals in France by origin region, 1946-1990**

National origin	1946	1954	1962	1968	1975	1982	1990
Belgium and Germany	10.2	9.1	5.7	4.1	2.9	2.6	3.1
Italy, Portugal and Spain	44.5	46.2	51.7	56.3	49.9	38.7	31.1
Other Europeans *	34.0	23.8	14.8	11.1	7.6	6.3	6.5
Total Europe	88.7	79.1	72.2	71.6	60.7	47.6	40.6
North Africa	2.3	12.9	18.9	23.6	32.2	38.8	38.7
Other Africa	0.8	0.1	0.8	1.2	2.3	4.2	6.7
Others	8.2	7.9	8.1	3.6	4.8	9.4	14.0

Note: *   Citizens from Austria, Britain, Bulgaria, Czechoslovakia, Denmark, Finland, Greece, Hungary, Ireland, Luxembourg, Netherlands, Norway, Poland, Rumania, Sweden and Yugoslavia.

Source: Derived from INSEE (1992)

(at around 0.4 per cent a year). The style of immigration has also changed, for it has become more family based, as established immigrants have brought their immediate relatives to live with them (Frybes, 1992). Significantly, then, British in-migration has been occurring at a time when the basic flow of new foreign residents has slowed down. This makes the contribution of British citizens to the total in-migrant flow more significant than its relatively small numbers might otherwise suggest. However, the role of British inflows is further distinguished by its contrast with both the character and the destinations of previous rounds of immigration.

Dominant immigrant nationalities

This is the case even though immigration has been dominated by intra-European movements. In the nineteenth century, this largely meant Belgians and Italians, who respectively accounted for 31.2 per cent and 31.9 per cent of all foreigners in 1901. Well into the twentieth century, the Italians continued to be the largest group of immigrants (accounting for 29.7 per cent of the foreign population in 1931), although in the immediate postwar years Polish nationals were present in significant numbers (accounting for 24.3 per cent of all foreigners in 1946). Traditionally, German and Spanish migrants have been in the second division of immigrant flows, with Spanish numbers experiencing a short-lived boost during the 1960s; when economic crisis in the late 1950s induced the Franco Government to encourage Spanish emigration (Wright, 1977). With a substantial overseas population being a long held feature of the Portuguese economy (Brassloff, 1993), the rise in the Spanish population to 20-23 per cent of all foreigners brought a heavy southern European flavour to the immigrant population. Today, while still representing about a third of all foreign residents (Table 3.2), this southern European contingent has declined significantly. Indeed, intra-European movements now make a much smaller contribution to the total foreign population. Europeans have been replaced, first and most consistently, by migrants from the three north African states with the strongest historical and economic links with France (Algeria, Morocco and Tunisia). More recently, their position has also been diluted by immigration from central Africa and Asia (in the latter case, mostly from Cambodia, Turkey and Vietnam). As a result, just 40.6 per cent of foreign residents in France now come from Europe, with Africans accounting for 45.4 per cent. Clearly, then, the immigrant hinterland of France has moved substantially outward from its position of 100 years ago, with its closest northern neighbours having ceded their place to ever distant lands, be they in southern Europe, Africa or Asia.

What adds to the diversity of the French population is not simply the variety of nationalities that are present within it but also the fact that periods of migrant inflows have been linked with dissimilar origin points. Hence, the long established Italian population is now relatively aged, and as newly arrived Italians are rare today, few Italian children now reside in France. By contrast, the more recent Moroccan population is notable for the size of its school age population (Festy, 1993).

This broad picture can be refined considerably if we examine the arrival of new foreigners during the last intercensal period 1982-1990. In total, some 605,211 foreigners were identified in the 1990 census as having arrived since 1982 (Table 3.3). It is notable that EC citizens still represent the largest group of newcomers (26.0 per cent against 23.5 per cent from the Maghreb states), yet the percentage of recent arrivals from Europe was much lower than the representation from this continent in the total foreign population (comprising 32.0 per cent of 1982-1990 immigrants, compared with 40.6 per cent for all foreigners in France in 1990). Indeed, the total number of non-French EC nationals declined from 1,963,590 in 1975 to 1,311,892 in 1990. Yet recent additions to the EC population are distinguished from other nationals because a relatively high proportion are economically active (Table 3.3). Thus, 54.1 per cent of EC migrants who entered France between 1982 and 1990 were economically active, compared with 31.5 per cent for the Maghreb population. Clearly, two different immigration patterns are operating. Immigration that originates in central Africa and the Maghreb is essentially limited by government policy to family members joining established workers. Intra-EC migration, by contrast, is more overtly work oriented.

But on closer examination we see that it is inappropriate to treat EC nationals in an undifferentiated manner. Hence, decline in EC representation between 1982 and 1990 was chiefly due to a fall in Italian, Portuguese and

Table 3.3   **Foreigners newly resident in France by region of origin, 1982-1990**

Region of origin	Migrants		Economically active migrants		
	Number	% of total for France	Number	% of all migrants	% of active migrants
All	605 211	100.00	256 888	42.44	100.00
EC nationals	157 561	26.03	85 258	54.11	33.18
Other Europe	34 719	5.73	17 698	50.97	6.88
Maghreb	142 571	23.55	44 962	31.53	17.50
Other Africa	89 412	14.77	35 676	39.90	13.88
Asia	137 416	22.70	56 936	41.43	22.16
Other	43 532	7.19	19 088	43.84	7.43

Source: Derived from INSEE (1992)

Spanish numbers (Table 3.4). Growth was recorded for north European states, and particularly for Britain, Denmark, Ireland and the Netherlands. Thus, the north European representation of 14.1 per cent of non-French EC citizens in 1990 was a substantial gain on its 9.5 figure in 1982. The polarity that is evident in these migration trends is important, for it raises the prospect that there are different motivations in the migration decisions of incoming citizens from the north and from the south of the EC. If this is so, then the geographical distribution of immigrants within France should differ between these two groups. This suggestion is strengthened when we examine the occupations that immigrants fill after they reach France.

Immigrant economic activities

The French literature stresses that the work roles of most immigrants are manual and blue collar; as well as being concentrated in particular industries, such as construction (Mottin, 1992). This pattern finds broad parallel with trends in other advanced economies (Fielding, 1993); although a peculiarity of the French situation is the low number who enter farming, which is probably explained by France's traditionally over-populated agricultural sector. Thus, while the farming sector includes 2.7 per cent of French families, [1] it accounts for only 0.4 per cent of the foreign population. By contrast, blue collar workers account for 20.4 per cent of French families but 47.4 per cent of non-French families.

Table 3.4   The EC population of France by country of origin in 1982 and 1990

	Number in 1982	% of EC total in 1982	Number in 1990	% of EC total in 1990	% change 1982 - 1990
All foreigners	3 714 200	-	3 596 602	-	-3.2
EC total	1 594 776	100.0	1 311 892	100.0	-17.7
Belgium	52 636	3.3	56 129	4.3	6.6
Britain	34 000	2.1	50 422	3.8	48.3
Denmark	2 216	0.1	3 544	0.2	59.9
Germany	44 000	2.8	52 723	4.0	19.8
Greece	7 812	0.5	6 091	0.5	-22.0
Ireland	1 716	0.1	3 542	0.3	106.4
Italy	340 308	21.3	252 759	19.3	-25.7
Luxembourg	3 304	0.2	3 040	0.2	-8.0
Netherlands	14 324	0.9	17 881	1.3	24.8
Portugal	767 304	48.1	649 714	49.5	-15.3
Spain	327 156	20.5	216 047	16.4	-34.0

Source: Derived from INSEE (1992)

With immigrants from individual north European nations comprising a small proportion of the total foreign population, published statistics relating to the economic activities of foreigners tend to distinguish only Italian, Portuguese and Spanish nationals within the EC total. Our attempts to discern the finer detail of immigrant economic activities, particularly amongst northern Europeans, have met with limited success. As a consequence, all we are able to offer here is a rather crude distinction between the three most prominent southern European states and the rest of the EC. Except for Greece, nations in the 'rest of Europe' are 'northern', but Greece contributes only 0.2 per cent of all resident foreigners in France, just 0.4 per cent of the non-French EC population and only 3.1 per cent of the 'northern' EC population. As a result, this division is a fair proxy for distinctions between northern and southern Europeans.

What is clear from this division is that the economic activities that are associated with these two European populations are different (Table 3.5). Service and tertiary sectors dominate the work roles of north European migrants, but the southern European position is overshadowed by the construction sector, which employs few north Europeans. In effect, the employment structure of northern Europeans resembles that of the domestic population (Table 3.5); which certainly is not the case for those from

Table 3.5   **Percentage of new immigrants to France in different economic sectors, 1982-1990**

	Total for France	EC 1	EC 2	Maghreb	Other Africa	Asia
Services	23.30	35.06	24.44	30.03	42.34	26.96
Industry & energy	22.48	20.30	13.24	13.31	14.22	47.20
Commerce	12.21	10.73	7.29	11.09	8.57	12.88
Construction	6.57	3.50	31.38	14.23	6.03	3.08
Transport	6.56	3.57	2.23	3.44	4.63	2.57
Agriculture & fishing	5.85	3.58	6.15	10.11	0.33	1.07
Others	22.97	23.26	15.28	17.79	23.88	6.25

Note: EC 1   Belgium, Britain, Denmark, Germany, Greece, Ireland,
                 Netherlands and Luxembourg.
          EC 2   Italy, Portugal and Spain.

Source: Derived from INSEE (1992)

southern Europe. In fact, southern European immigrants, along with those from Africa and Asia, help fill occupational niches that are not highly prized by the domestic population, and so prime social mobility for French citizens (Le Bras, 1993). The same cannot be said for northern Europeans. It follows that those who come to France from northern Europe should be distributed geographically in a dissimilar manner from their southern European counterparts.

The geographical distribution of immigrants

At one level, the geography of immigrant destinations in France has been remarkably stable over the last 100 years. The north east, east and south, together with the cities of Paris (in the Ile de France region), Lyon (in Rhône Alpes) and Marseille (Provence Alpes Côte d'Azur) are the principal foci for immigrants today (containing some 60 per cent of all foreigners); as they were in 1891 (Le Bras, 1993). In terms of first points of arrival, migrant destinations have long been distinguished by the issue of proximity; as with the arrival of Spaniards in Toulouse, Bordeaux and the south west, Italians in Lyon and the south east, and both Belgians and Germans in the east and north east. As the migration hinterland of France has extended outwards over time, this basic premiss has changed little; with north Africans tending to head first for cities on the Mediterranean coast (Labat, 1992). Indeed, while there has been a gradual spread of immigrant groups over the last 100 years, generally this has not taken the immigrant population much beyond the aforementioned geographical zones (Harnois, 1992). In some regions of

Table 3.6   **Percentage of foreigners in local populations by size of commune, 1975-1990**

		1975	1982	1990
Rural communes		2.7	2.2	2.0
Urban communes	Under 5000 inhabitants	4.5	4.0	3.6
	5 000 - 9 999	5.5	5.2	4.7
	10 000 - 19 999	5.9	6.0	5.7
	20 000 - 49 999	6.4	6.9	6.5
	50 000 - 99 999	6.3	6.9	6.8
	100 000 - 199 999	7.1	7.3	6.5
	200 000 - 1 999 999	7.5	7.9	7.0
	Paris	12.0	13.9	13.7
France		6.5	6.8	6.3

Source: Harnois (1992)

France, like Brittany, the north west and parts of the Massif Central, the number of immigrants has been consistently low. However, so broad a geographical assessment does not highlight changes in distribution that have occurred in recent years. These are closely linked to the changing composition of immigrant populations and to the motivations that have brought more north Europeans to France.

Dominant immigration flows in France continue to follow the traditional pattern of regional concentration and urban destination (Table 3.6). However, at a time of decline in the foreign population (Table 3.1), the regions that registered growth between 1975 and 1990 are significant. Apart from Ile de France, [2] growth occurred in 11 of the 22 regions of France (Alsace, Aquitaine, Bretagne, Basse Normandie, Centre, Haute Normandie, Limousin, Pays de la Loire, Picardie and Poitou-Charentes). Of these, only five registered growth in the 1982-1990 period (Bretagne, Centre, Haute Normandie, Pays de la Loire and Picardie), with numbers in Alsace, Basse Normandie and Poitou-Charentes remaining stable. What is significant about these growth regions is that they were largely ignored by traditional immigrant flows. Their recent emergence suggests either that existing foreign residents in France are changing their home location or else that new immigrants are targeting western and north western regions. We obtain some support for the latter hypothesis when we recall the increasing importance of north Europeans in the French population and compare their geographical distribution (Figure 3.1) with those from southern Europe (Figure 3.2) and from outside the EC (Figure 3.3). Here we find that a small number of départements have concentrations of north Europeans that are well above average, at the same time as their contingent of other foreigners

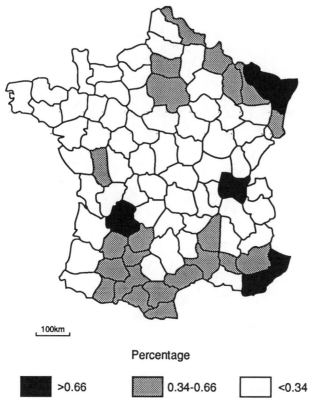

Percentage

■ >0.66   ▧ 0.34-0.66   □ <0.34

Figure 3.1　　　**Percentage of 'northern' non-French EC residents in the population of each département in 1990**

is well below the national average. Most evident in this regard are Alpes de Haute Provence, Ardèche, Ardennes, Aude, Bas Rhin, Dordogne, Garonne, Hérault, Lot, Meuse, Nord, Pyrénées and Tarn et Garonne (the location of these départements is given in Figure 2.2). As Figure 3.1 shows, these départements are distinguished either by their western location or by their rural character (or both).

British immigrants in France

As Chapter One revealed, among those northern Europeans who have been attracted to France in recent years, there has been a rapid growth in the number of British nationals (Table 1.2). This growth is 'officially' recorded in government counts, like the census or the issuing of the French residency

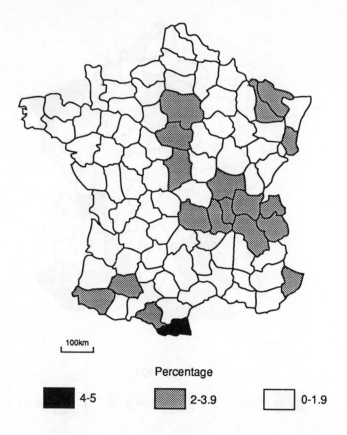

Percentage

■ 4-5   ▨ 2-3.9   □ 0-1.9

Figure 3.2   Percentage of the population in each département that were Italian, Portuguese or Spanish in 1990

permit, the *carte de séjour* (e.g. Ministère de l'Interieur, 1991; INSEE, 1992). However, because there is no national record of those who live in France on a seasonal basis, or who 'neglect' or fail to appreciate the need to register, it is clear that official figures underestimate the real number of north European residents. Most evidently, this is suggested by the assessments of those who are directly involved in or comment upon the French property market (e.g. de Warren and Nollet, 1990). Yet it must be stressed that property based estimates are not grounded in a systematic data base, for while the Chambre Interdépartementale des Notaires de Paris is establishing a data base that will eventually enable it to identify all property acquisitions (and sales) by non-French citizens, at this time the computerization of these records has not progressed sufficiently to give accurate figures on foreign property ownership. As such, for the clearest indication of changes in the north European population, we must still rely on official counts that exclude most second home owners.

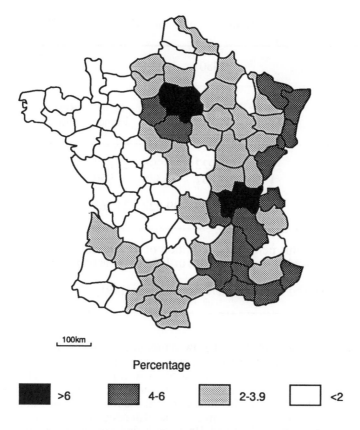

■ >6   ▓ 4-6   ▒ 2-3.9   □ <2

Figure 3.3   **Percentage of the population in a département that were not EC citizens in 1990**

Amongst these more permanent residents from northern Europe, the British population is second only to that of Denmark and Ireland in terms of its rate of increase over the last census period (and both these nations started with far smaller numbers; Table 3.4). Britain supplied the largest absolute increase in newcomers over between 1982 and 1990, as well as recording the largest percentage increase in its share of the total non-French EC population (with a 1.7 per cent gain). Furthermore, as a contributor to the economically active foreign population, since 1982 Britain ranks second amongst EC nations (INSEE, 1992), in addition to making up the largest national group of permanent salaried workers from Europe [3] that have entered France since 1983 (INSEE, 1992, p.128). Hence, in 1990, some 2,421 permanent salaried workers entered France from Britain. This was 10.8 per cent of the permanent salaried workers that came from all countries in that year and was well ahead of the numbers from Germany (1,403), Italy (1,978) and Portugal (822).

Table 3.7   **British holders of a *carte de séjour* in 1980 and 1991**

	1980			1991		
	Ile de France	Rest of France	Total	Ile de France	Rest of France	Total
Adults	18 374	17 922	36 296	22 613	33 131	55 744
Children *	1 339	1 987	3 326	1 950	4 347	6 297
Total	19 713	19 909	39 622	24 563	37 478	62 041

Note: Over this period the definition of a child did change. In 1980 it referred to those under 16, in 1991 to those under 18.

Source: Derived from Ministère de l'Interieur (1991)

However, once we move below national aggregates, to establish the geographical spread of British migrants, we find that census data does not differentiate British migrants from other north Europeans. To separate British citizens from nationals of other countries, we have to turn to data supplied by the Ministère de l'Interieur on those foreigners who hold a *carte de séjour*. [4] These more 'permanent' British residents grew in number by 57 per cent between 1980 and 1991, with this growth displaying a clear preference for the more rural départements of western France that lie some distance away from major urban centres (Figure 1.1). That British migrants are not moving to the traditional foyers of immigrant installation in France is readily displayed by the declining importance of Paris and the Ile de France as a British reception area. This region accounted for 50.6 per cent of all adult holders of a *carte de séjour* in 1980, yet by 1991 its representation amounted to just 40.5 per cent. Significantly, this regionalization is particularly noticeable for children (Table 3.7), which suggests that families who move to France with young children increasingly avoid Paris and the Ile de France.

Outside the Ile de France, the recent evolution of British *carte de séjour* holders has not been spread evenly (Figure 1.1); nor have in-migrants gone to the more traditional areas of British residence. For a long time now, certain coastal départements have attracted British settlers. Coastal zones in the Provence Alpes Côte d'Azur region (PACA), for example, became popular retreats for the British social elite in the nineteenth century (viz. the famous *Promenade des Anglais* at Nice), while the Channel ports of Calais and Dieppe have longstanding enclaves of British nationals (in the past playing host to such diverse figures as James Thackery and Oscar Wilde). Yet while the départements of the PACA and the Nord regions accounted for

29.7 per cent of British *carte de séjour* holders who lived beyond the Ile de France in 1980, by 1991 this had fallen to 24.0 per cent; even though there had been an overall increase of 88.0 per cent in British numbers outside the Ile de France. It is true that some individual départements in these historically important regions continue to have many British *carte de séjour* holders (e.g. 3,520 in Alpes Maritimes, 1,615 in Var and 1,573 in Nord, against an average of 416 for départements beyond the Ile de France), but over the last decade their growth rates have been much lower than départements which previously had a slight British occupancy. Thus, while Bouches du Rhône (PACA) registered a growth of only 5.3 per cent, three French départements had growth rates of more than 500 per cent, four of between 400 and 500 per cent and a further seven recorded at least a 300 per cent rise. The result was that the number of départements with at least 500 British *carte de séjour* holders increased from 11 in 1980 to 23 in 1991, while the number with at least 300 went up from 19 to 41.

By taking rates of growth in British numbers, alongside the proportion of all British *carte de séjour* holders that live in a département, we find four 'regional' types. These can be referred to as traditional areas of British settlement, growth areas, areas with a stable British contingent and areas with a declining British residential role. Traditional areas of British settlement are essentially those départements that had a considerable British presence in 1980. While these départements did register some growth in British numbers between 1980 and 1991, this growth was not translated into an increase in their share of the total British population of France. Départements that fall into this category include Alpes Maritimes, Dordogne, Isère, Nord and Var. Those places that we define as growth départements registered the largest increases in British numbers over the 1980 to 1991 period, despite the fact that the total number of British residents might still be small in comparison with traditional areas of British occupation. Départements that stand out in this regard are most prominent in western and southwestern regions, such as in Basse Normandie, Brittany, Languedoc Roussillon, Limousin, Midi Pyrénées and Poitou-Charentes. Such areas contrast with those places that reveal stable British numbers, largely because this latter group has not experienced the rapid rise in British intake of their western counterparts. Amongst these 'stable' areas, more northerly and easterly regions are prominent, with départements in the Alsace, Centre, Champagne Ardenne, Haute Normandie and Lorraine standing out. Finally, in a small number of cases, areas have seen their contingent of British *carte de séjour* holders decline (e.g. in Ardennes, Corse, Haute Loire and Meuse). For the most part, départements in this category house small numbers of British citizens. Pas de Calais is one exception, as the number of British *carte de séjour* in this département remains at well above the mean average figure for départements outside Ile de France (standing at 582 in 1991).

These broad geographical trends confirm that the general thrust of British movement into France in the 1980s has been toward western and, virtually by definition, more rural départements. As an illustration, the département with the largest 1980-1991 percentage increase in British *carte de séjour*

51

Table 3.8   **British *carte de séjour* holders by commune size in Sarlat arrondissement, Dordogne, 1990**

	Commune size	Number	% of total
Rural communes	Under 50 inhabitants	0	0.00
	50 - 99	2	0.70
	100 - 199	34	12.05
	200 - 499	112	39.71
	500 - 999	71	25.17
	1 000 - 2 000	26	9.21
Urban communes	(over 2 000)	37	13.12
Total		282	100.00

Source: Derived from *carte de séjour* files, Préfecture de la Dordogne

holders was Corrèze, which is often held to be one of the most traditional rural départements of France (Béteille, 1981). Even in single départements, the role of rural destinations is demonstrable. Thus, in the arrondissement of Sarlat in Dordogne, [5] British *carte de séjour* holders reveal a marked bias toward living in small rural communes (Table 3.8).

The British contribution to the population geography of France is quite different from that of immigrants from Africa, Asia and southern Europe. It remains to be shown whether British destinations also differ from those of other northern Europeans. Comparing British *carte de séjour* holders with their Dutch and German equivalents, for these are the next biggest north European groups in France, we find départements with relatively high 1991 representations of each nationality group. Most prominent in this regard were Alpes Maritimes, Dordogne, Nord and Var, as sites with a strong British and Dutch presence, with Alpes Maritimes and Haute Garonne also featuring amongst the top five départements for German *carte de séjour* holders (although the three most populous German départements, Moselle, Bas Rhin and Haut Rhin, hardly feature as British destinations; Table 3.9). Clearly, there are similarities in the locational choices of British, Dutch and German nationals. Yet, apart from Alpes Maritimes, whose attractive mountain landscapes and suitability for skiing is an obvious attraction (Figure 3.1), only four départements exert a particular pull on citizens from all three nations (Bouches du Rhône, Hérault, Nord and Var). All of these are coastal locations, as well as being longstanding centres of in-migrant flows.

Even so, British *carte de séjour* holders are distinguished from their north European neighbours in two particular ways: first, they have a stronger representation in more rural départements; and, second, since 1980 their number has grown in a precipitous manner compared with their Dutch

Table 3.9   Départements outside Ile de France with the most British, Dutch and German *carte de séjour* holders in 1991

British		Dutch		German	
Département	Number	Département	Number	Département	Number
Alpes Maritimes	3 520	Alpes Maritimes	1 384	Moselle	7 506
Var	1 616	Hérault	600	Bas Rhin	5 518
Nord	1 573	Dordogne	568	Haut Rhin	2 580
Haute Garonne	1 487	Bouches du Rhône	491	Alpes Maritimes	2 004
Dordogne	1 456	Var	442	Haute Garonne	1 712
Hérault	1 213	Nord	345	Nord	1 643
Ain	1 187	Ardèche	295	Var	1 421
Bouches du Rhône	1 186	Ain	292	Bouches du Rhône	1 314
Gironde	1 048	Gard	276	Rhône	1 103
Rhône	928	Gironde	248	Hérault	989

Note: Information for the Dutch population of Haute Garonne is not available.

Source: Ministère de l'Interieur (1991)

and German counterparts (Figure 3.4). Thus, if we exclude the Alpes and the Côte d'Azur, it becomes apparent that Dutch and German nationals have generally concentrated in different parts of France from one another. For the Dutch, a broad southerly strip running from the Ardèche in the south east toward the Pyrénées stands out, while Alsace records the highest German concentrations. The former of these zones has attracted some British interest, but at a less intense level than départements on the north western edge and even somewhat further north of this belt. Alsace is far removed

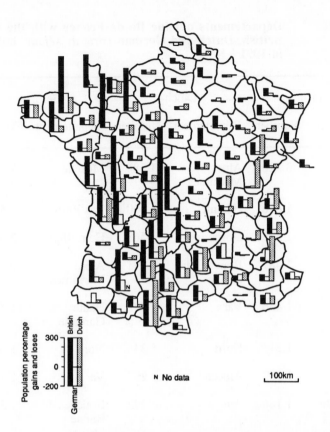

Figure 3.4   **Percentage change in British, Dutch and German**
carte de séjour **holders in each département, 1980-
1991**

from the British sphere, for it attracts very little attention from British buyers
(e.g. Figure 1.2). In addition, British citizens are distinguished from Dutch
and German nationals by their fourfold increase in various départements
between 1980 and 1991. For the Dutch, so high a percentage gain was
recorded only once (in the département of Ariège in the Pyrénées) and it was
never reached by the German population. Thus, whereas mean average rates
of growth over this period for Dutch and German *carte de séjour* holders in
départements outside the Ile de France were 37.0 and 32.0 per cent, for the
British the figure was 88.0 per cent. Particularly in western France, rates of
increase for British *carte de séjour* holders stands well above the figures
recorded for Dutch and German nationals (Figure 3.4). Indeed, from the
northerly Breton département of Côtes d'Armor right down to Gers in the
south west (Figure 2.2), there was an almost continuous band of

54

Table 3.10   British *carte de séjour* holders and other nationals in the five study areas

	Foreign citizens as a % of the total population	British *carte de séjour* as % of foreign citizens	Northern EC [1] (1990)	Southern EC [2] (1990)	Other foreign citizens (1990)
			Per cent of all foreigners		
Calvados	1.81	5.31	26.81	21.56	51.63
Charente Maritime	1.37	7.25	15.56	39.73	44.71
Dordogne	2.86	13.13	24.80	38.59	36.61
Lot	3.20	12.80	18.56	51.52	29.92
Vaucluse	7.79	1.24	5.75	23.86	70.39
France less Ile de France	4.82	1.68	6.25	31.68	62.07
France total	6.34	1.72	5.38	31.10	63.52

Note: 1   Belgium, Britain, Denmark, Germany, Greece, Ireland, Luxembourg and The Netherlands.

2   Italy, Portugal and Spain.

Source: Ministère de l'Interieur (1991) and INSEE (1992)

départements which at least doubled their number of British *carte de séjour* holders between 1980 and 1991 (Figure 3.4).

Foreigners amongst foreigners in five départements

Up to this point, we have identified both the current growth in the number of British migrants in France (against a background of overall immigration decline) and the current destinations of newly resident British *carte de séjour* holders (which are distinguishable from those of other national groups by their markedly rural focus). Before going on to consider British nationals as property buyers, rather than simply as immigrants, we wish to look in closer detail at the immigrant population of the French départements in which we have undertaken questionnaire surveys of British property owners (information on the methodology of this work can be found in Hoggart and Buller, 1993a). These five départements are Calvados (in the region of Basse Normandie), Charente Maritime (Poitou-Charentes), Dordogne (Aquitaine), Lot (Midi Pyrénées) and Vaucluse (Provence Alpes Côte d'Azur). They were selected for more detailed investigation both because they represented the range of circumstances under which British households were purchasing a rural French home, so they cover areas with a variety of physical and social characteristics (see Hoggart and Buller, 1993a) and include coastal locations (as with Calvados and Charente Maritime), some of the more remote rural areas of the south west (as in Dordogne and Lot), as well as the Provençal département of Vaucluse, whose southern border lies just north of the Mediterranean.

In terms of their foreign population, these départements fall into three groups. The coastal départements of Calvados and Charente Maritime have the smallest foreign contingent, with both falling well below the 4.8 per cent average for départements beyond Ile de France (Table 3.10). Britons and other northern EC nationals are over represented in these départements, but other foreigners, [6] notably those from the Maghreb nations, are significantly under represented. Dordogne and Lot form a second group, for the British percentage of their foreign populations is among the highest in France. Like Calvados and Charente Maritime, Europeans constitute the dominant foreign population here, with Lot also having a longstanding southern European population. Also like Calvados and Charente Maritime, non-Europeans in these départements are significantly under represented. Vaucluse contrasts with the other four départements in three important ways. First, Britons form a relatively minor group amongst the resident foreign population (1.2 per cent). As a proportion of the total they are certainly under represented compared with the national average, while in real numbers they are less numerous (at 454 *carte de séjour* holders) than in the four other départements (Calvados 596, Charente Maritime 525, Dordogne 1,456 and Lot 640). Secondly, the foreign resident population of Vaucluse is dominated by an urban based North African contingent (Table 3.10). Thirdly, in general, foreigners make up a larger proportion of the economically active population than in the other départements. Thus, 7.0 per cent of the active population of Vaucluse is comprised of foreigners, compared with percentages of 1.6 in Calvados, 1.4 in Charente Maritime, 2.5 in Dordogne, 3.0 in the Lot and 4.5 for all the départements lying outside the Ile de France (INSEE, 1992). Linked to this is the high proportion of foreigners who are actively engaged in agriculture. While this figure stands at 5.3 per cent for non-Ile de France départements (and for the other four départements investigated is 2.9 per cent in Calvados, 5.7 per cent in Charente Maritime, 14.0 percent in Dordogne and 8.2 per cent in Lot), the figure for Vaucluse reaches 32.2 per cent. This high number is a reflection both of the dominant type of agriculture in this département (fruit plantations), which necessitates a large, albeit often seasonal, workforce and of the fact that the south east of France is a traditional destination of Maghreb nationals (George, 1986b).

Together, these figures suggest that there are important differences in the function of French residence for migrant populations in the départements we investigated. Calvados and Charente Maritime can be characterized as playing host to a small foreign population that is not economically active in the main, that is largely of north European extraction and which is of

Table 3.11   Purchases of rural land in Calvados by nationality of buyer, 1989-1991

Country of origin	1989	1990	1991
France	870	839	781
Britain	162	101	56
Other EC nations	18	6	10
Other nations	14	15	14
Total	1 064	961	861

Source: Direction Régionale de l'Equipement de Basse Normandie (1992)

relatively recent installation. At the other end of the scale lies Vaucluse, with a large foreign population (over 1.0 percent of all foreigners in France), which is largely economically active and non-European. Dordogne and Lot take intermediary positions, as longstanding hosts to northern Europeans (who are often not economically active) and an economically active southern European group.

The British as house buyers in rural France

A combination of rapidly increased numbers and a focus on western and southern France made British buyers significant players in rural housing markets in the late 1980s (Hoggart and Buller, 1994c). In some départements there was a history of British property owning (notably Alpes Maritimes, Dordogne and Nord), but the general rise in British property acquisitions in the late 1980s was a spectacular one. After 1990 sales did decline but property agents point to them picking up again in 1993 (Hoggart and Buller, 1993b). Yet it was the sharp rise in sales in 1988 that attracted a range of French commentators, from academics (e.g. Levesque, 1993), to state agencies (e.g. Direction Régionale de l'Equipement de Basse Normandie, 1989), journalists (e.g. Simonnot, 1991) and commercial interests (e.g. Crédit Agricole, 1991). What was significant about this interest was that it was stimulated not by the presence of British nationals amongst the French population but by the impact of British purchases on rural property markets.

The boom of 1988-1990

Precise figures at the national level concerning the acquisition of French property by British nationals are regrettably non-existent. However, using a variety of different local sources, the very existence of which bears

57

Table 3.12   Annual mean average purchases of rural land by foreigners in Dordogne, 1990-1991

Country of origin of buyer	Total area (hectares)	Per cent of total area purchased
Belgium	2 320	14.3
Britain	6 380	39.3
Germany	1 480	9.1
Italy	300	1.8
Netherlands	410	2.6
Non-EC Europeans	3 260	20.1
Others	2 050	12.8
Total foreign acquisitions	16 200	100.0

Source: SCAFR (1993a)

testament to local awareness of the phenomenon and the need to understand its size and future direction, we are able to piece together a clear picture of the sudden explosion of British buyers onto the French property market during the 1988-1990 period. These sources fall into the two broad groups. One the one hand there are popular writings and journalistic accounts, while on the other hand there are reports by state or local government agencies and by economic consultancies. All these information channels point to a phenomenal growth in foreign acquisitions by northern Europeans in general and by the British in particular in the late 1980s (Anon, 1988; Genet, 1988; Gardère, 1991; SAFER de Basse Normandie, 1991; Direction Régionale de l'Equipement de Basse Normandie, 1992; see Table 3.11). Indeed, whereas 15 years ago it was Belgian and Dutch nationals who dominated foreign purchases of French rural property, by the end of the 1980s the British were the principal foreign investors; accounting for around 40 per cent of all buyers of rural property (Levesque, 1993). Illustrative of this trend, in the four Breton départements of Côtes d'Armor, Finistère, Ille et Vilaine and Morbihan, purchases by British nationals of rural buildings and vacant land accounted for 90.6 per cent of all acquisitions by foreigners over the two years 1988 and 1989; a period that saw the total number of property purchases by foreigners rise from 321 to 1,515 (Cellule Economique de Bretagne, 1990). Similarly, in the three south western départements of Dordogne, Lot et Garonne and Tarn et Garonne (Figure 2.2), Britons represented 81.4 per cent of foreign buyers of rural property, 8.9 per cent of all buyers and 20.4 per cent on all non-farmer buyers (SOGAP, 1990). Likewise an analysis of foreign buyers in 10 rural communes in the département of Tarn found that 86.0 per cent were British (Bages

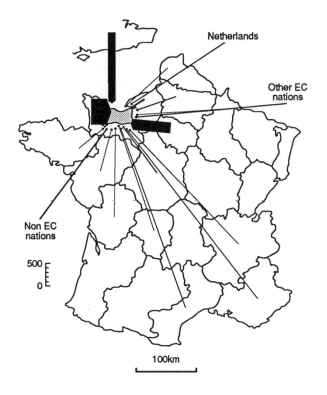

Figure 3.5   **Origin regions for buyers of built rural properties in the Vire arrondissement of Calvados in 1989**

were British (Bages and Puech, 1993). Finally, in a synthesis of regional land transactions for DATAR, [7] the British were identified as the principal non-agricultural buyers of rural land in France (Table 3.12). Our own analysis confirms this picture, as seen in 83.5 per cent of all foreign buyers of rural property in Calvados and 15.2 per cent of all buyers in 1989 being British; with their principal competitors from outside Basse Normandie coming from the Paris region (Figure 3.5).

Commentators confirm that British involvement in the French property market was relatively feeble before 1988, took off during 1988 and 1989 and began to decline in 1990. Indicative of increased British purchases, in Nord-Pas de Calais, British acquisitions of second homes rose from 30 in 1987 to 230 in 1988 and to over 500 in 1989 (Defrenne, 1990), while the Chambre des Notaires de la Seine Maritime points to 45 purchases in 1988, 131 in 1989 and 62 between the 1 January and 30 September 1990 (Fonatine, 1990). According to Crédit Agricole, in Seine Maritime, 90 to 95 the homes owned by Britons in 1990 had been bought since 1988 and 90 per cent of these were second homes (Lettre, 1990). Elsewhere, we have considered the role of both British and French estate agents in responding to and directing British demands toward French rural property (Hoggart and Buller, 1992a; Hoggart and Buller, 1992b; Buller and Hoggart, 1993; Hoggart and Buller, 1994a). These reports confirm both the scale and the periodicity of British behaviour in this market, for French estate agencies from a variety of regions report that three quarters or more of their 1989 clients were Britons, whereas only a quarter or so came from across the Channel in 1992 (Buller and Hoggart, 1993). What further distinguishes the boom of 1988-1990 is the fact that so many of the regions that previously attracted British interest had property markets that were slow moving. As a result, as the number of British buyers increased, so did the number of property transactions in these départements (Buller and Hoggart, 1993; Hoggart and Buller, 1993b). In the same way, as the number of British acquisitions has fallen, so too has the total volume of property sales (Table 3.11).

As identified in Chapter Two, in the late 1980s awareness of the residential attractions of rural France increased greatly, with changing house prices in Britain providing a financial stimulus that enhanced this appeal. Foremost among the attractions of rural France were property availability and the 'genuine' character of the expected rural 'experience'. Both of these are linked to the large number of homes that lie vacant or under used in remoter areas of rural France; owing to a lack of buyer interest amongst local populations. The explosion of British buyers onto French rural property markets confirmed that availability but added other explanatory factors. The following two chapters, based upon our survey of 406 British home owners in France, seeks to identify the character and relative importance of these other factors.

Notes

1   This definition is based upon the profession of the head of household.
2   The Ile de France comprises the départements of Paris, Seine et Marne, Yvelines, Essonne, Hauts de Seine, Seine Saint Denis, Val de Marne and Val d'Oise.
3   Permanent salaried workers have permanent salaried employment and hold the relevant work permit.
4   A *carte de séjour* is a residence permit, awarded by the Prefecture of the département of residence, that all foreigners require if they stay in France for more than three months at a time.
5   The arrondissement is a local electoral unit made up of a number of cantons, themselves made up of individual communes. There are usually four or five arrondissements in a département.
6   The basis for identifying these different national groups is not the same for all. The British population is identified by the number of *carte de séjour* holders in 1991, while the others are identified

through published INSEE population statistics derived from the 1990 census.

7 DATAR is an abbreviation for Délégation d'Aménagement du Territoire et d'Action Régionale, which is a state regional planning agency.

4 Buying a French home

The preceding chapters have spelt out three main features of British house buying in France. The first is that the volume of home acquisitions rose significantly in the late 1980s, although it has since fallen back somewhat, with both of these temporal trends showing strong links to the buoyancy of British housing markets. The second is that the British show a clear preference for buying in rural areas, where there is an abundance of old and often disused properties, that are not only cheap by British standards but also meet idealized British images of the rustic country cottage. In their rural distribution, British buyers reveal a third important attribute, which is the uniqueness of their locational decisions compared with those of other non-French EC citizens. What provoked this geographical distribution is the core issue for this chapter. In addressing this question we will be drawing largely on the questionnaires that were completed by our 406 household survey respondents [1]. In doing so we will analyze their responses in the context of key distinctions between property buyers. The first of these is obviously whether the home was purchased during or after the boom in French home acquisitions that occurred in the late 1980s, for the character of the British housing market and the information that was available to potential buyers were so different before and after this boom started. The second distinction concerns the use to which a home is put; for *a priori* we would expect that second home owners have different needs and aspirations in acquiring a French property than householders who change their main residence. Within these categories we would normally examine whether there were other factors that contributed to buyer differences, such as social class and whether householders are retired or not. However, there is little variation in the occupational standing of French property buyers (Table 2.4) and comparisons between different white collar occupations reveal few occupational distinctions of note. Moreover, we have shown elsewhere that there is little difference between retired and pre-retirement households for most aspects of house buying (Hoggart and Buller, 1994b).

Fundamental to our assessment of differences over time and between homes with different residential uses are the reasons people select a particular place for their French property purchase. This is important not only in terms of why France became the nation of home ownership, but also for the choice of a specific region in France and of a particular property within that region. If our primary argument holds good, then those who bought their homes during or after the 1988 boom (post-1987 buyers) should reveal a keen appreciation for the issue of prices in their purchase decision, as well as emphasizing aspects of rurality in their choice of property. Whether or not this distinction holds for first and second home owners is a moot point, for non-retired households at least. Yet, while we can expect pre-retirement households who move permanently to France to be conscious or even to be driven by income earning prospects, if our interpretation of the rationale for such moves is correct, then employment issues should still be of lesser importance than the attractions of cheap living and a rural lifestyle. Of course, it is feasible that geographical differences are important here. So, for each of the timing of property acquisition, the role that a French home play in the lifestyle of a household and regional location, this chapter analyzes reasons for selecting France, a particular département and a specific property.

Département, time of purchase and home use

Effectively, information from our survey on the département of home location and the timing of house purchase are contextual factors rather than population counts. In the former case this is because our survey sought a random sample of British home owners, rather than a census of British residents. In the latter case it arises because our investigation was not intended to identify British people who purchased a property in France but had sold it or died before 1992 (i.e. prior to our survey). Yet, while our insights are drawn solely from existing owners of a French property, the patterns they reveal are consistent with general trends in official statistics (as with changes in the number of British holders of a *carte de séjour* ; e.g. Figure 3.4). In addition, of course, our data offers insight on dimensions of British home ownership that are not hinted at in official records. As one illustration, a significant finding is that just under half of our respondents defined their French property as their first home (Table 4.1). Moreover, this percentage holds for all the départements we investigated. It holds when we exclude the three households that defined their two homes as being of equal importance to them (all of whom we list as second home owners), just as it does when we remove the nine households who now live in France permanently but whose French property was bought as a second home. It also applies when we control for the time of purchase. Thus, the percentage of all buyers whose property is a second home ranges from 52.3 to 59.2 for post-1987 buyers in four of our départements (once the above exemptions are made). Only Vaucluse stands apart, with a figure of 46.7 per cent. However, as we only obtained 32 questionnaire responses from this département, the addition of just two more second home owners would have placed this area firmly within the range of the other départements. Hence, when we make comparisons across départements, we compare places with roughly equivalent first and second home representations.

Table 4.1 **Percentage of British buyers in a département by time of property purchase and home role**

	Calvados	Charente Maritime	Dordogne	Lot	Vaucluse	All
Pre-1988						
First home	4.3	13.3	19.6	15.9	19.4	14.4
Second home	3.2	5.0	20.3	10.1	32.3	13.1
Post-1987						
First home	40.4	33.3	28.7	30.4	25.8	32.2
Second home	52.1	48.3	31.5	43.5	22.6	40.3
First home, all years	44.7	46.8	48.3	46.4	46.9	46.6

Source: Authors' survey

Such regional equivalence does not hold for comparisons of the timing of property purchase, for higher percentages of Dordogne and Vaucluse residents purchased homes prior to the late 1980s boom than in other départements (Table 4.1). This partially confirms our selection of these areas as places with distinctive British residential histories, but it also emphasizes the need to be conscious that comparisons across départements are influenced by such distinctions. This point should also be made for Calvados, where the scale of British inflow was meagre prior to the upsurge in demand in the late 1980s. Excluding this département, as it had so few pre-1988 buyers, first home owners only exceed their second home counterparts in three cases. Perhaps, for post-1987 buyers in Vaucluse this difference should be discounted, as the difference in first and second home representation is so meagre, yet the distinctions in pre-1988 moves to Charente Maritime and Lot are of some significance. Effectively, with no longstanding tradition of British home buying in these départements (unlike in Dordogne), early home purchases were more likely to be for permanent residence. Yet, during and after the 1988-1990 boom, along with Calvados, these areas had the highest rates of second home acquisition (compared with first home purchases); although these areas did record substantial first home acquisitions after 1987. Indeed, the increase in first home ownership in 'non-traditional' areas of British residence was actually greater than in more established zones of British occupation. Illustrating this, the 1989-1991 increase in *carte de séjour* holders was 97.4 per cent for Charente Maritime, 81.1 per cent for Calvados and 80.8 per cent for Lot, whereas the percentages for Dordogne and Vaucluse were just 49.5 and 26.4, respectively. Putting these different trends together, we find that 47.7 per cent of pre-1988 buyers are now second home owners (with 48.1 per cent buying their home as a second home), compared with 55.8 (and 57.3) per cent of post-1987 purchasers.

Significantly, though, provided no allowance is made for the date of home purchase, there is almost no difference in the incidence of first and second home owners across départements. Once allowance is made for the timing of home acquisition, then we find patterns do differ between areas of traditional British presence and places that have seen a more recent expansion in British interest. In order to explore the character of these differences, we need first to establish if they are based on dissimilar linkages with reception areas prior to home purchase.

Links with France

Previous residence in France

In all, 104 respondents had lived in France prior to buying their present French property (25.7 per cent), with the balance between current first and second home owners being equal. Yet many of these connections were reported to be distant ones. In addition, they were rarely with the département in which a property is now owned. Thus, of the 97 households for which accurate locations were obtained for a previous home, only 14 had lived in their present département before and only 10 had lived in an adjacent département. By contrast, 41 had lived in the Paris region at some point in the past. [2] Some inter-département differences were found here, with a higher rate of prior residence for those in Vaucluse (53.1 per cent). Yet the Vaucluse position is not matched by Dordogne, the other area of longstanding British occupation, where only 24.1 per cent of respondents had at least one household member who had previously lived in France. This low proportion is little different from the percentages for Charente Maritime (33.3), Calvados (21.8) or Lot (15.9).

If we add a temporal dimension to these figures, in every département, pre-1988 in-migrants were more likely to have lived in France before buying their home than later purchasers. It is true that for the two départements that have a stronger tradition of British occupation, this difference was marginal; with the percentages for Vaucluse at 56.2 for pre-1988 purchasers and 56.3 for post-1987 buyers (and 20.9 per cent and 27.6 per cent for Dordogne). Hence, while the magnitude of prior residential linkages with France is different for Dordogne and Vaucluse, these départements are similar in terms of the temporal stability of their linkages. By contrast, Charente Maritime recorded a fall from 63.6 to 22.4 per cent in the proportion of its pre-1988 and post-1987 buyers that had lived in France prior to occupying their present home, with notable falls also for Calvados (42.9 to 19.3 per cent). Amongst the non-traditional foci for British residence, only Lot, with its consistently lower rates of prior residential links, revealed slight temporal differences in prior residential connections with France (with percentages of 22.3 and 13.8 for pre-1988 and post-1987 buyers, respectively). Vaucluse apart, then, we cannot point to previous residence as a major factor that has encouraged British people to buy their present property in France. Perhaps earlier living experiences in France promote a positive attitude towards the idea of French home ownership, but most people have this irrespective of whether they have lived in France before. Moreover, 42.3 per cent of those with a previous residential history in France only lived in the Paris region, which probably means that their direct experience of life in rural France was little different from those who had only taken regular holidays there.

Enhancing the sense that a prior residential history was primarily important in establishing a positive orientation towards rural France, post-1987 first and second home buyers were little different in terms of whether they had ever lived in France before buying their present home (the percentages having done so were 20.3 and 22.5, respectively). These figures are smaller than their pre-1988 equivalents (at 40.3 and 30.7, respectively), but the greater likelihood of first home buyers having previously lived in France was not .05 significant in a chi-squared test.

Family and friends in France

As well as previous residence, a further mechanism through which knowledge and an appreciation of (rural) France could have been obtained is from contacts with friends and family in that country. Unlike previous residential history, a slim majority of our respondents did have kith or kin connections with France (50.8 per cent). As some of these connections would be formed during periods of residence in that country, it merits noting that 75.0 per cent of those with a previous French residential history had family or friends living in France prior to purchasing their present home, but only 42.5 per cent of other respondents did. In all, 42.7 per cent of our respondents reported that they had neither lived in France nor had friends or family living in France prior to the purchase of their present French home. In addition, at least as regards family relations, those linkages that did exist generally did not involve the strongest blood ties. For instance, amongst those with adult children who moved their main home to France, just 23.5 per cent of pre-1988 buyers and only 9.7 per cent of post-1987 purchasers had a child living in that nation prior to their home purchase. By contrast, for these two time periods, 73.5 per cent and 90.1 per cent of the same property buyers still had children living in Britain. If family ties encourage permanent home relocations, then it is to be expected that family connections in France will be even less prominent for second home owners. This is indicated by only 6.3 per cent having an adult child living in France (for retired second home owners the figure was 2.3 per cent).

If we broaden the linkage base to include all family members and all friends, we pick up another aspect of the peculiarity of post-1987 first home buyers. In the previous section we recorded that this group was the least likely to have a previous French residential history. When examining kith and kin ties, we find that they also have the weakest ties with France. In fact, just 42.1 per cent of these respondents had family or friendship ties with France prior to home purchase, as compared with 51.2 per cent for post-1987 second home buyers. Also consistent with evidence on residential histories, those who purchased their homes before 1988 were more likely

Table 4.2   **Percentage of first home owners with French kith or kin links prior to home purchase**

Year bought	Calvados	Charente Maritime	Dordogne	Lot	Vaucluse	All
Pre-1988	*	63.6	56.1	61.1	66.7	58.7
Post-1987	49.4	42.9	39.5	58.8	62.5	47.8

Note: Only four first homes were bought in Calvados before 1988, so it would be misleading to calculate a percentage for this table.

Source: Authors' survey

to possess such ties before they came to France; although first and second home owners were little different in this regard (recording percentages of 59.6 and 57.7, respectively). Again, we can identify differences across départements, with Vaucluse recording the strongest connections and both Charente Maritime and Lot revealing particularly strong local links amongst pre-1988 buyers (e.g. Table 4.2). In combination with the evidence on residential histories, the picture that is emerging is of earlier purchasers having stronger ties with France, with this effect being particularly pronounced in Vaucluse. Also of note, amongst those who purchased their home after 1987, was that first home purchasers had weaker prior linkages.

Visiting France

Quite feasibly, these first home owners did have significant prior connections with France, but these were less 'formal' than residential or family and friend ties. Two obvious possibilities in this regard are holidays in France and visits to that nation for other reasons (both were assessed in terms of visits within the five years immediately prior to property purchase). Here we focus on both of these aspects, with visits to France being evaluated in terms of those that were made to the département in which a home was eventually bought. Restricting the definition of visits in this way reduces any exaggeration that could result, quite legitimately, from people passing through France to other continental destinations or making innumerable short stay trips for business purposes to a single French contact. The critical messages from this information are that 40.7 per cent of all purchasers had not visited the département of their French home in the five years before they undertook steps to acquire their present property, with 17.4 per cent not having taken a vacation in France during this period. If we focus on those who had both no prior residential history in France and no family or friends living in that nation, we find that 45.3 per cent had not visited the

Table 4.3   **Percentage of British buyers with no holiday in France or visit to their département of residence in the five years prior to home purchase**

	Pre-1988 buyers		Post-1987 buyers	
	First home owners	Second home owners	First home owners	Second home owners
Holiday in France				
Never	26.4	12.8	25.4	9.2
Once	7.5	2.1	13.9	7.9
Visit département				
Never	46.3	26.5	46.0	36.9
Once	9.3	6.1	16.7	20.4

Source: Authors' survey

département in which they bought their home in the five years prior to property purchase (with a further 41.8 per cent having visited it less than once a year), while 17.6 per cent had not taken a holiday in France in these five years (a further 17.1 per cent had less than annual holidays there). Yet, while many households did not have particularly strong linkages with France before they bought their home, it can be said of few that they had no connections with that nation at all (just 7.2 per cent of all our respondents had no residential history, no family or friends, no holidays and no visits to their home département in the run up to home acquisition).

But if we wish to understand the evolution of British home ownership in France, we need to consider whether differences are distinguished by date of purchase or home use. However, the further we go back in time the more likely that any contrast between purchase dates will be a comparison of chalk with cheese, given that the ease, real cost and time available for foreign travel have changed so significantly over the last four decades. It follows that those who purchased their property in the 1940s, 1950s or even 1960s cannot be expected to have had as much opportunity for foreign travel as later buyers. However, what has compensated for this tendency has been the growing awareness of the possibility and potentials of French home ownership. This has undoubtedly encouraged those with more tenuous connections with France to contemplate the possibilities of overseas home ownership. One result is that differences over time are less than one might expect. Thus, while the percentage of first home owners who had not visited the département of their home in the five years prior to purchase was 61.5 per cent for those buying a property before 1980, this had fallen to 32.1 per cent for 1980-1987 buyers, only to rise to 46.0 per cent for post-1987 owners (Table 4.3). For holidays the picture is very similar, with the percentage of first home owners who had had no holiday in France in these five years standing at 34.6, 18.5 and 25.4 for each of these time periods. Clearly, then, the boom in French home acquisitions in 1988 was significant in that it drew people with relatively weak prior connections with France; reversing the trend toward acquisition based on stronger associations with that country.

Before leaving this point, obvious issues to address are differences by home use and social class. Of course, one might predict that these are related, with second home ownership and foreign travel being less likely amongst those of lower income in earlier decades. However, when we break down our first and second home owners by occupation, we find that all bar higher education lecturers saw a greater percentage owning a second home after 1987. In the case of manual workers and artisans, however, these changes were minor, with both having many more first home owners than second home buyers. Yet examination of these two groups does not indicate that temporal change is critical, for the percentage pre-1988 buyers who had not visited their département of residence was 60.0 for manual workers and 44.4 for artisans (with 0.0 and 22.2 for no holiday in France), compared with figures of 63.2 and 34.4 for post-1987 buyers (with 38.9 and 19.0 for no holiday). This points toward first and second home ownership as the more important divide. To examine this issue in more detail comparisons were made within occupation groups. Being the largest group in absolute numbers, as well as being representative of the general trend, the figures for school teachers are instructive. Here, taking the percentage who had not visited their département in the five years before they purchased their home, we find almost no temporal change, with pre-1987 and post-1988 proportions of 50.0 and 48.4 for first home owners and 30.0 and 30.4 for second home owners (with figures for buyers in the 1970s and early 1980s showing no major differences). The extraordinary point though is the continuing pattern of first home owners having fewer connections with France than those who have bought a second home. Moreover, although the proportion of first home owners hardly differs across our five départements, we again note substantial place disparities in prior connections with this nation. For purchasers in Calvados, for example exactly half had not visited this département before they began to look for a property in it. The figures for Charente Maritime (44.9 per cent), Dordogne (35.7 per cent) and Lot (39.6 per cent) are slightly lower, but Vaucluse again stands apart with only 20.0 per cent of respondents not having visited the area in the five years before they bought a home there. Quite evidently, in Vaucluse there is a more enduring connection between British buyers and France than in the other départements.

Property agent effects

Elsewhere we have focused on the role of property agents in selling French homes to British people. We have dealt with company organization and entry into this housing market in Britain (Hoggart and Buller, 1992a) and in France (Buller and Hoggart, 1993), as well as analyzing the advertising campaigns (Hoggart and Buller, 1992b) and roles of these companies in market development (Hoggart and Buller, 1993b, 1994a). In a paper that focuses explicitly on the effects these companies have in directing buyers toward particular types of housing and to particular geographical areas, we concluded that their most notable impact was seen in the way they heightened awareness and interest in French property ownership amongst Britain people (Hoggart and Buller, 1994a). However, we also identified an ability of agents, in limited circumstances to be sure, to direct or attract potential buyers to locations which they might otherwise not have considered. In this context there is a clear temporal effect, as most British companies in this market were started after the 1988 boom (Hoggart and Buller, 1992a). This boom also took French estate agents and notaires by surprise, so they initially relied on British firms to market their properties (Buller and Hoggart, 1993). Only in a few areas, such as Dordogne, was there an 'established' marketing link between Britain and France when the rapid expansion in British interest occurred. This meant that early British buyers had comparatively little marketing assistance when finding areas for home acquisition. Nevertheless, the advertising campaigns of companies, the needs of which have produced a number of specialist British magazines on French property (like *Focus on France*, *French Property Buyer*, *French Property News* and *Living France*), together with the media attention they received, did raise the tempo of British interest (Hoggart and Buller, 1994a). Effectively, this acted as a strong information flow that eased paths toward purchase for later buyers; as in informative articles on planning, taxation, inheritance laws or obtaining work, that regularly appear in French property magazines.

The question this raises, given that first and second home owners are differently connected with France prior to property purchase and that differences exist between départements, is whether intended home use and the département of home location were linked to the way households found their property. If second home owners and those buying in Vaucluse tended to have stronger linkages to France, does this mean that they relied less on property agents? The answer for both groups is yes (Table 4.4). Acknowledging the dominance of temporal effects in this relationship (only 12.1 per cent of pre-1988 buyers found their home through an agency in Britain, compared with 39.3 per cent of later purchasers), we find that 47.2 per cent of post-1987 first home owners relied on agencies whereas only 32.9 per cent of second home buyers did. That there was little difference between these groups in the propensity to find properties on their own, merely confirms that second home owners have stronger connections with France. This arises because the other chains that drew householders to their French home were dominated by information from friends or relatives in France.

For differences across départements, Vaucluse again stands apart, with none of our respondents identifying their home from a connection that started in Britain (Dordogne also has a low figure for recent second home purchasers). At the other extreme, Charente Maritime comes across as the area that is most dependent on company advertising in Britain; which no doubt owes much to the newness of this area as a site of British interest, along with the considerable attention that companies have given it in their

Table 4.4   **Percentage of post-1987 buyers identifying their property through an agency or by themselves**

	Calvados	Charente Maritime	Dordogne	Lot	Vaucluse	All
By agency						
First home	44.7	55.0	29.3	25.0	0.0	47.2
Second home	35.4	51.7	15.9	39.3	12.5	32.9
By self						
First home	50.0	35.0	63.4	50.0	62.5	52.0
Second home	52.1	37.9	61.4	46.4	100.0	52.5

Note: 'By agency' is where buyers identified their property through adverts or information provided by a company which they obtained in Britain. 'By self' refers to finding a property when travelling in France.

Source: Authors' survey

promotion campaigns (its unique combination of coast, nature reserves and picturesque inland towns being commonly stressed). Such positive advertising is not restricted to Charente Maritime, but also extends to Lot, as well as to parts of northern France, like Brittany and Normandy (including Calvados). Indeed, it seems highly likely that property magazines and newspaper articles have been instrumental in heightening and broadening the appeal of these areas, at least in so far as they allay fears about their accessibility to Britain for second home owners (e.g. Anon, 1990b). Publicity undoubtedly helps explain the significant increase in second home ownership that has occurred in more southerly départements since the 1988 boom started (Table 4.1). However, areas like Charente Maritime have also been promoted through an emphasis on their cheap house prices (Hoggart and Buller, 1993a). But consideration of this aspect of property acquisition takes us into the realm of why householders selected the home they bought. This is what we turn to in the next section, taking with us the themes of distinct differences between pre-1988 and post-1987 buyers, of dissimilarities in first home and second home owner linkages, and of the disparities between areas that have a stronger tradition of British residence, like Dordogne and, particularly, Vaucluse, and more recent places that have attracted British interest.

Opting for France

Evaluations of France as a home location involve both absolute and relative assessments (housing in France is cheap fullstop and housing in France is inexpensive relative to Britain). For most of our respondents, relative evaluations involved comparing France with Britain alone. A central position for Britain in such evaluations is to be expected, as just 10.2 per cent of our informants had a home outside Britain at the time they purchased their French property. However, this does not preclude them from considering nations other than France for home purchase. Yet the centrality of British-French comparisons is evident in the small number of respondents who considered a nation other than France. In all, only 28.6 per cent considered buying a home elsewhere (the figure was 31.7 per cent for those living outside Britain), with only four nations being considered by a sizeable number of households. Spain was at the top of this list, with 9.8 per cent considering it, with Britain (7.0 per cent), Italy (5.3) and Portugal (5.0) also recording potential buyer interest. The British figure is particularly significant, for when we break down responses by time of home purchase and by home use, we find that only post-1987 first home buyers had more than 7.0 per cent of their members considering Britain (with 11.8 per cent). With figures of 5.2 per cent for all second home owners and 4.6 per cent for all pre-1988 buyers, this suggests that these groups of home purchasers saw few prospects of obtaining a suitable property in Britain. Indeed, for second home owners, just 22.6 per cent considered a nation other than France, compared with 35.1 per cent for those who relocated their main home. Moreover, while pre-1988 purchasers were more likely to consider France alone, this tendency was still stronger amongst second home buyers (82.7 per cent, as against 70.2 per cent), as it was for post-1987 purchasers (75.0 per cent against 63.0 per cent).

Whatever the time period and however the home was to be used, the majority considered nowhere except France. This indicates that buyers generally felt that France offers something that other nations do not. The slight consideration that second home owners gave to other nations points in the direction of price, given the extra cost of maintaining two homes. But it is possible that a simpler explanation exists, in the form of dissimilar linkages with France prior to property purchase. Table 4.5 illustrates that some linkage patterns do distinguish first and second owners, although having previously lived in France and having family and friends already living there appears to be the only two linkages that bind first home owners more strongly to that nation. The former of these is interesting because prior residence in France had the opposite effect on second home owners. However, on inspection, this only applies for those who bought their home after 1987 (for whom 18.8 per cent who had not lived in France considered another nation for their home, compared with 30.8 per cent that had lived there). Again, then, we can point to the distinctive behaviour of second home owners who purchased their property after the late 1980s boom began.

When set against differences between first and second home owners, cross département distinctions are easily understood, for the patterns we

Table 4.5   **Percentage of British buyers who only considered buying in France and who considered other nations**

Attributes of householders	First home owners		Second home owners	
	Only looked at France	Considered another nation	Only looked at France	Considered another nation
Lived in France before	30.8	16.7	22.0	31.3
Kith or kin in France	52.9	37.9	53.3	52.1
Have an adult child in France	9.2	4.5	1.8	8.3
No retired members	53.3	53.0	77.4	77.1
No visit to département	40.0	54.5	35.8	32.6
No holiday in France	20.8	30.3	10.3	8.9

Note: The categories 'No visit to département' and 'No holiday in France' both refer to the five years prior to home purchase.

Source: Authors' survey

have already identified were confirmed. Thus, Vaucluse residents had the strongest ties to France (just 18.1 per cent considering buying in another nation) and Calvados owners had the weakest (34.7 per cent considering elsewhere), with the others standing at 29.0 per cent (Charente Maritime), 28.7 per cent (Dordogne) and 24.2 per cent (Lot).

This distribution across départements does not mean that dissimilarities between them are critical in understanding British buyer behaviour. For one thing the reasons why people choose a nation can be quite different from their rationale for selecting a particular region within that nation; although the possibility of interaction effects between the two should not be ignored. However, when we look at the reasons householders gave for buying in France, the main factors they mentioned include few issues with a strong regional flavour (Table 4.6). In truth, the notable aspects of these reasons relate to what people did not consider as well as with what they did. [3] In particular it is worth recording that employment related reasons were not significant. Indeed, from the various cross tabulations we computed, moving to France for a job or business opportunity was mentioned by more than 10 per cent of respondents on only two occasions (the 12.3 per cent of first home buyers who acquired their home before 1988 and 12.5 per cent of Vaucluse residents). Amongst the factors that were mentioned, various points distinguish first from second home owners, as well as differentiating earlier and later buyers. Many of these, however, were not distinctions of

Table 4.6　　　**Percentage of British buyers naming specific reasons for selecting France for a home**

| | Pre-1988 buyers | | Post-1987 buyers | | |
	First home owners	Second home owners	First home owners	Second home owners	All
Property prices	14.0	5.8	39.1	26.4	25.4
A Francophile	28.1	23.1	18.0	27.7	24.0
Access to Britain	8.8	21.2	15.6	34.0	23.0
Liked climate	17.5	26.9	22.7	21.4	21.5
French lifestyle	19.3	3.9	18.8	13.8	14.8
Could speak French	10.5	17.3	9.4	15.7	13.1
Former home here	15.8	15.4	10.9	2.5	9.1
Took holidays here	5.3	3.9	7.0	10.1	7.7
Family reasons	19.3	7.7	5.5	4.4	7.2
Liked food & drink	0.0	9.6	8.6	7.5	6.9
Liked the area	8.8	9.6	4.7	6.3	6.4
Liked the people	1.8	3.9	7.8	8.2	6.4
Left UK long ago	14.0	7.7	8.6	0.6	5.9
Liked rural areas	5.3	3.9	7.8	4.4	5.4

Note:　These responses were from an open ended question, not a checklist. The table lists reasons given by at least 5.0 per cent of respondents.

Source:　Authors' survey

magnitude, as with the greater tendency for second home owners to select France because of their knowledge of the French language (Table 4.6).

Most fundamental, both in terms of their overall importance and the manner in which they distinguished household groups, were the role of property prices, access to Britain and an appreciation of the French lifestyle. Describing yourself as a Francophile and liking the 'French climate' were also influential, but these did not separate the main household groups. In temporal terms, the most influential distinction was that of property prices. In response to an open-ended question on reasons for selecting France, just 10.0 per cent of pre-1988 buyers mentioned property prices, yet 30.9 per cent of later purchasers did. There is no doubt that this distinction is aligned to the rise in house prices and the ready availability of credit in Britain over the 1988-1990 period (Chapter Two). However, we should also note the effects of the media in sensitizing potential buyers to the availability of cheaper homes in France. Indeed, in our interviews with companies that sell property in this market, considerable criticism was raised over media emphasis on house prices; for it was felt that potential buyers are too easily led into believing they can buy a home that needs no attention for very little money. If this is the case, it seems likely that it has affected first home buyers the most, for they were more attracted by cheaper properties than second home owners both before and after the start of the 1988 boom (and property prices were more significant for households with no retired members than those of retirement age, as seen in the 31.8 per cent of pre-retirement respondents mentioning cheap house prices, as compared with 13.8 per cent for retired). This is not the point to examine inter-relationships between household characteristics in depth, for our understanding of the role of property prices in attracting British buyers is deepened by investigation of reasons for selecting a particular département and a specific home. However, one further division should be noted, which is variation across départements. Here, we find that property prices were much more influential in Calvados than anywhere else (42.1 per cent), with just 3.0 per cent of Vaucluse respondents mentioning this factor and the others ranging from 19.4 to 27.4 per cent.

The peculiarity of Calvados in this regard comes across in two other ways. First, perhaps not unexpected given that it is the only northern département in our study, few Calvados residents were attracted to France by its climate (4.2 per cent); with climatic considerations not being distinguished by other household features (e.g. Table 4.6). Then, following the same pattern as house prices, access to Britain was approximately twice as important for Calvados residents (at 40.0 per cent) as it was for the three middle ranking départements, with Vaucluse buyers regarding this as a matter of slight importance (9.1 per cent). In this case we see a simple distance to ferry port effect, yet the access issue is also more important for second home owners (and especially for post-1987 purchasers). Again we would expect this based on *a priori* reasoning. Also to be expected, perhaps, is the distinguishing behaviour of early first home owners, for whom important decision criteria included family considerations (including marriage) and movement to France after a long absence from Britain. These owners also revealed a notable attachment to the French lifestyle, but this was shared with later first home buyers.

We can summarize the most pertinent information on reasons for selecting France for home purchase by stressing four points. The first is that few buyers considered a nation other than France, which points to particular features of this country attracting British interest. The second is that the reasons people gave for electing to buy in France were numerous, with no single factor being dominant. This raises the third issue, which is the varied character of purchasing groups. First and foremost we see this in the much greater importance of property prices amongst those who acquired a home during or after the 1988 boom. Also of note is the differential importance of access to Britain and of people's appreciation of the French lifestyle, for both had dissimilar roles in the decisions of first and second home owners. Then there is a distinct pattern amongst early first home buyers, with family connections or periods away from Britain being notable considerations. As our fourth point, we must draw attention to cross département differences.

Table 4.7 Percentage of British buyers naming specific reasons for selecting a département for a home

| | Pre-1988 buyers | | Post-1987 buyers | | |
	First home owners	Second home owners	First home owners	Second home owners	All
Liked climate	22.8	30.8	28.1	30.8	28.6
Access to Britain	3.5	13.4	25.0	31.4	23.7
Liked scenery	22.8	23.1	20.3	23.9	22.7
Liked rural areas	14.0	19.2	18.0	22.0	18.8
Property prices	15.8	5.8	19.5	13.2	14.3
Knew the area	15.8	19.2	10.9	10.7	12.3
Had local friends	14.0	9.6	7.8	9.4	9.6
Liked the house	8.8	0.0	7.8	8.2	6.9
Liked the area	3.5	5.8	4.7	9.4	6.7
Access to water	0.0	9.6	7.0	6.9	6.4
Liked the people	8.8	5.8	3.1	7.5	6.2
Few British people	5.3	3.9	4.7	6.9	5.7
Regional lifestyle	8.8	7.7	4.7	4.4	5.4

Note: These responses were from an open ended question, not a checklist. The table lists reasons given by at least 5.0 per cent of respondents.

'Access to water' refers to the sea, a river or a lake.

Source: Authors' survey

In some measure, as with access to Britain and climate, these merely reflect the geographical position of our study areas. However, to appreciate these differences, we need to take our argument further, by investigating reasons for selecting a particular département and a specific home.

Selecting a département

As with choosing France itself, the majority of British property owners considered just one French département for their home purchase (40.6 per cent considering more than one). Evaluation of the options that were considered reveal geographical concentrations in buyer interest. For Calvados owners, for example, 62.1 per cent only considered this département, with a further 18.1 per cent raising the possibility of buying elsewhere in Normandy or in Brittany (Hoggart and Buller, 1993a). This northwestern focus was matched by a southwestern one for those who eventually bought in Charente Maritime, Dordogne or Lot, with the Aquitaine region accounting for 66.7 per cent of places that Charente Maritime owners considered outside this département. The neighbouring départements of the Midi Pyrénées region took up 54.5 per cent of places that Lot residents considered beyond their eventual home département. As for Vaucluse, here we find the highest proportion who did not look elsewhere (66.7 per cent), although this is not far ahead of Calvados and Dordogne (60.1), with Lot (57.6) and Charente Maritime (51.6) not so far away. Otherwise there was no notable concentration in the places evaluated by Vaucluse residents, with the regions of Aquitaine, Languedoc Rousillon, Midi Pyrénées and the remainder of Provence Alpes Côte d'Azur all being considered by around 10 per cent of Vaucluse buyers. Most likely their broad geographical spread owes much to stronger prior links with France; with the importance of Paris in earlier residential histories also having a role, given that prior city residence is less likely to result in searches for a rural home being directed toward specific locations in the countryside.

The reasons why specific départements were selected for home acquisition are different from the factors that attracted buyers to France. At one level these differences are expected, for many of the criteria that led people to buy in France do not distinguish between places in that nation. Being a Francophile, being able to speak French and having an appreciation of 'the French lifestyle' are three criteria of this kind; all of which were among the top six reasons that respondents gave for selecting France. Even so, three of the top six factors in the choice of a département were also among the first six reasons for selecting France; albeit at the département level the relative importance of these factors was not the same as for national choice (Table 4.7). Thus, climate shifts from the fourth to the most important criteria as we move from the national to département scale. Access to Britain also increases its relative importance by moving from third to second place, although property prices significantly decline from first to fifth rank. Moreover, in the appearance of 'scenery' and rurality in the top six decision criteria, we begin to see the significance of the rural dimension in French property acquisition. Perhaps more significantly, however, many of the divisions that exist in reasons for buying a home in France, such as when the property was purchased and whether it is a first or a second home, are not manifest in the criteria the households used to select a département. Indeed, when we examine the four housing groups that so clearly distinguished reasons for selecting France, the only decision criteria that was different for pre-1988 and post-1987 buyers was the greater importance that post-1987 buyers attached to access to Britain (Table 4.7). As for distinctions between first and second home owners, here no divisive decision criteria emerged with conviction (certainly none come close to statistical significance in chi-squared tests). Not unnaturally, our attention is thereby drawn to potential differences across the five départements we studied.

Here we find that the decision criteria that were influential at the national level are enhanced in département selection. The importance of climate, for instance, remains insignificant in Calvados (8.4 per cent naming it as a factor in département selection), but its importance intensifies for Charente Maritime (with 56.5 per cent defining as a primary criteria) and Vaucluse (45.5 per cent). Working in the opposite direction, access to Britain reaches major heights as a determinant of purchases in Calvados (at 66.3 per cent), which means that residents of this area comprised 65.6 per cent of all respondents who gave accessibility as a decision criteria (although Calvados residents comprised just 23.7 per cent of our respondent sample). Such is the power of this Calvados effect that when we exclude it from consideration, post-1987 second home owners are the only group for which at least 10 per cent of its members saw the accessibility issue as a key to their selection of a département (at 16.3 per cent), with other combinations of purchase date by home use recording percentages that ranged from 1.9 to 8.2.

What we begin to see here is differences between départements in purchase decisions that has little to do with the reasons that prompted people to buy in France. Indicative of this, just 30.1 per cent of those who placed a high regard on climatic factors in national or département selection did so for both, with the comparable figure for access to Britain at 28.9 per cent. The lesser role of property prices in département selection, compared with reasons for choosing France, also indicates that key reasons for drawing buyers to France were not central when they looked for a specific property within that nation. As such, at the level of the département, we should look for distinct geographical dimensions in the decision criteria of British buyers.

Evidence of this effect is not difficult to find, as Charente Maritime buyers reveal. For these informants, the primary attractions of their département were its warm climate, alongside a notable emphasis on access to the sea (19.4 per cent). In addition, this was the only département that was selected by more than 10 per cent of respondents because its British population was believed to be very small (17.7 per cent). Otherwise, there were similarities between the decision criteria of its residents and those of Lot (another area of recent British inflow). Not only do both report that property prices were significant in département choice (21.0 and 24.2 per cent, respectively), but they also record the highest incidence of rurality as a positive attraction (30.6 and 33.3 per cent). In terms of differences between these two départements, we find that respondents in Charente Maritime provided responses with a stronger 'sun and sand' orientation, while those in Lot were more inclined to point to the drawing power of the local scenery (24.2 per cent, compared with 6.5 per cent for Charente Maritime). With a higher proportion of Lot residents reporting that they knew the area before purchase (16.7 per cent, compared with 6.5 per cent), and with more emphasis on the attractions of a specific house (12.1 per cent) or local food and drink (10.6 per cent), it is clear that the kind of rurality that is sought by British residents in these two départements is different.

In so far as we can characterize Lot buyers as being attracted by a more 'traditional' rural landscape, compared with their more 'sun drenched' Charente Maritime equivalent, British owners in this département were attracted by similar factors as those who moved to Dordogne. In reality, when we selected Lot as a study site, we were directed to it by interviews with estate agents and government officials which suggested that there would be differences with Dordogne. These differences were expected to arise because some households found property prices in Dordogne too expensive. As a consequence, they were said to be rejecting Dordogne, in favour of cheaper but scenically similar areas in Lot. Yet just 13.8 per cent of our Lot respondents reported that they seriously considered buying a home in Dordogne (with 6.3 per cent of Dordogne buyers considering Lot). Of course, it is possible that people became sensitive to Dordogne prices before seriously investigating this département (either through reading or from property agent advice). Certainly, Lot residents were more likely than Dordogne buyers to report that property prices were significant in département choice (24.2 per cent as compared with 9.0 per cent). Yet, while we expected a stronger Dordogne inclination to report that family and friends were important attractions (given the stronger tradition of British residence in this département), in fact only 17.9 per cent of Dordogne residents named this factor, which is not so different from the figure of 11.6 for Lot. Moreover, while it appears as though rurality was a critical discriminator between these two places, with only 13.1 per cent of Dordogne residents naming it as a key attraction (compared with 31.9 per cent in Lot), on closer examination we find overlap in the importance of scenery and rurality. Thus, twice as many respondents in Lot than in Dordogne linked scenery explicitly to the countryside (as opposed to architecture, for instance). This weakens the distinctiveness of responses in these two départements in some measure, but not sufficiently to remove them. Just as Calvados attracted those who were more concerned with access to Britain, and Charente Maritime drew greater attention from those who sought sun and sand, Lot residents must be distinguished from those of Dordogne by their greater emphasis on traditional rural landscapes (as opposed to scenery *per se*) and, in some measure, by price.

As for Vaucluse, apart from the question of climate that we have already referred to, this département occupies a similar position in buyers' minds as Dordogne. Access to Britain is of little importance (6.1 per cent), as are property prices (3.0 per cent). Regional scenery is weighted in the same manner as in Dordogne (24.2 per cent), as is the rural character of the area (12.1 per cent) and previous knowledge of the département (12.1 per cent, with Dordogne at 18.6 and Lot at 15.9). Climate apart, then, this leaves few major differences between these two départements, although more residents of Dordogne (17.9 per cent) than of Vaucluse (6.1 per cent) were drawn by family or friends in their new locality. Yet, on the reverse side, 21.2 per cent of Vaucluse buyers were attracted by a friendly local population, which only 5.5 per cent of Dordogne buyers mentioned. Possibly these effects cancel one another out, so leaving climatic attractions as the principal discriminator between these two places. However, we should also recall the stronger French connections of eventual Vaucluse buyers; which perhaps leads them to have a broader appreciation of the character of their recipient département.

Certainly, we should note that when selecting a département, more than 40 per cent of our respondents had not visited this area in the five years prior to looking for a property (if ever). Moreover, only 4.0 per cent gave employment related reasons for choosing a département. Even if we object that this is a false figure, given the presence of retirees and holiday home buyers in our sample, there is no doubt that job related moves were of slight importance. Take pre-retirement first home owners alone and you still find only 12.1 per cent giving an employment reason for département selection. If this points to the dominance of consumption issues in the choice of a département, then this view can only be intensified when we note the lack of difference in the criteria used by first and second home buyers. Moreover, the features that drew most people to places, like the climate, the scenery, rurality and access to the sea, provide a strong indication that consumption interests were crucial in département selection. And these interests are set amidst a framework in which property prices were a primary factor that pulled post-1987 buyers toward France, with few considering a nation other than France. Both trends are consistent with the themes we developed in previous chapters about the linkage between British interest in France and the 'thwarted' or 'unrealizable' goals of middle class Britons. But, for a book with counterurbanization in the title, at this point little has emerged in home selection criteria about the rural base of our investigation. This is to be expected. After all, anyone who wants to live in a rural area and is comparing the relative merits of Britain, France and Italy does not start by contrasting specific villages. Rural areas are no more unitary than are cities (Hoggart, 1990). In the same way, when we consider the areas our respondents assessed for house purchase, with Aquitaine, Bretagne and Midi Pyrénées figuring most strongly (with French estate agents only adding Provence Alpes Côte d'Azur to this list in their assessments of areas of acute British interest; Figure 1.2), we can see that British eyes are focused on areas with broad expanses of open countryside. It follows that strong statements about rural living are not to be expected when we consider reasons for national and regional choices. Where we should find such sentiments is in the key characteristics that attract householders to specific properties.

Choosing a home

This expectation is readily confirmed when we examine the reasons informants gave for selecting their French home (Table 4.8). The two single criteria that stood above others, in terms of their significance as criteria in home purchase decisions were the desire for an isolated, peaceful rural location and the attractions of scenic views from the home (or at least of the home being located in a generally scenic neighbourhood). The latter of course does not have to refer to rural areas, but respondent comments were punctuated with references to the rural character of the scenery that attracted them. Then again, caution is perhaps necessary because our survey areas in Calvados and Dordogne where geographically concentrated, so they contained few settlements with more than 2,000 inhabitants, whereas respondents in the other three départements were randomly selected. Yet the extent to which responses from Calvados and Dordogne emphasized rurality was not appreciably different from the other départements. In fact, only in Vaucluse did the proportion of informants who stressed their preference for an isolated, rural location fall outside the 38.9 to 43.8 per cent range (again

Table 4.8   **Percentage of British buyers naming specific reasons for selecting a particular French property**

	Pre-1988 buyers		Post-1987 buyers		
	First home owners	Second home owners	First home owners	Second home owners	All
Isolated, rural area	35.1	42.3	33.6	47.2	40.2
Liked scenery	35.1	48.1	38.3	35.2	38.0
Character property	19.3	23.1	25.0	25.8	23.7
In/near village	19.3	13.5	21.1	23.9	21.5
In good condition	12.3	9.6	19.5	23.3	18.8
Large property size	15.8	13.5	16.4	13.8	14.8
Property price	10.5	17.3	18.8	10.7	13.8
Central to region	12.3	5.8	18.0	13.8	13.6
A property to restore	8.8	19.2	10.2	11.9	11.6
Large land area	0.5	1.9	18.8	8.2	10.9
Access to water	3.5	5.8	10.9	11.3	9.6
Just the right house	8.8	3.8	14.1	5.7	8.4
Local facilities good	3.5	3.8	7.0	8.2	6.4
Liked local people	8.8	11.5	4.7	5.7	6.4

Note: These responses were from an open ended question, not a checklist. The table lists reasons given by at least 5.0 per cent of respondents.

'Access to water' refers to the sea, a river or a lake. 'Just the right house' refers to a combination of specific factors making a particular property suited to a household.

Source: Authors' survey

using an open-ended question). Such a difference is readily understandable given the settlement geography of this département, in which there is a limited range of dwellings in the open countryside, with higher concentrations in villages. Hardly surprising, then, that 48.5 per cent of Vaucluse responses gave being in or just outside a village as a key property attraction, whereas the figures for the other départements were much lower (the highest was Charente Maritime at 32.3 with the other three départements in the 13.2 to 20.0 per cent range). Indeed, when we examine differences across départements, the most notable distinction is the weight

Table 4.9   **Percentage of British buyers for whom property or rurality issues dominated home choice**

	Calvados	Charente Maritime	Dordogne	Lot	Vaucluse	All
Property only	24.0	22.5	21.3	15.9	6.1	20.0
Rurality only	14.6	9.7	23.3	26.1	39.4	20.9
Both	54.1	59.7	50.7	55.1	42.4	53.0
Neither	7.3	8.1	4.8	2.9	12.1	6.2

Source: Authors' survey

placed on scenic beauty, where Dordogne, Lot and Vaucluse all had between 44.8 and 47.8 per cent of respondents emphasizing this factor, whereas in Calvados (28.1) and Charente Maritime (22.6) the percentages were much lower. Already we have identified the strength of access to Britain (Table 4.7) and of cheap property prices in drawing people to Calvados (Table 4.6), with sun and sand being significant drawing cards for Charente Maritime (Table 4.6; Table 4.7). What attitudes towards landscape scenery suggest is that these considerations were dominant for these buyers, so the 'necessity' for 'their rurality' to have picture postcard qualities was a lesser consideration than elsewhere.

This being the case, we can expect Calvados and Charente Maritime home owners to place more weight on property features in their purchase decisions than buyers in other départements. To assess this we aligned the reasons respondents gave for home selection into three groups; namely, those related to the property itself, those related to rurality and other reasons. When we distinguish those who only gave property based reasons, we find that Calvados and Charente Maritime buyers do stand apart as more property oriented (Table 4.9); although this is largely evident in the lesser weight householders gave to rurality alone. In truth in all départements save Vaucluse, both property features and rurality were important to more than half our respondents (Table 4.9). In Vaucluse, rurality, which was largely expressed in terms of a village location, received more weight than anywhere else, with property issues being of much less importance. This might be linked to the slight role that Vaucluse residents gave for property prices, as well as to the greater leverage that prior knowledge of this area had on the interest of these buyers. Effectively, those who chose Vaucluse were more likely to have been drawn by their knowledge of its specific character, rather than by a desire for a particular type of property.

This summary needs to be tested in the context of potential differences between groups of home buyers, lest this département effect is closely aligned with the timing of home purchase or the intended use of a property. In fact, there were few difference in the proportion of first and second home owners across our five départements, but the same is not true for the timing of property purchases (Table 4.1). Yet, while the primary reasons for buying a home in France have changed over time (Table 4.6), few of these distinctions were carried into precise property selection. In fact, of the main decision criteria that buyers used in home selection, just three revealed temporal distinctions and these were not strong (Table 4.8). In the case of later buyers placing more weight on their property being in a good condition, the explanation probably lies in property magazine and newspaper reports which have indicated that the costs and potential problems of property renovation are much greater than British people generally assume (Hoggart and Buller, 1993a). In the case of earlier buyers placing more weight on the friendliness of the local people, this probably results from their stronger links with the area prior to purchase, as seen in more pre-1988 purchasers having kith or kin links with a département prior to buying a home there (Table 4.2). As for post-1987 buyers being more attracted by proximity to water, here we are seeing the effect of the later growth of purchasing activity in Charente Maritime and, to a lesser extent, Calvados; for both of these areas have the biggest proportion of post-1987 buyers and they are the only départements in which more than 10.0 per cent of respondents claimed that access to water was critical to their property selection (with 22.6 per cent of Charente Maritime buyers viewing this as a prime attraction).

More notable than these temporal distinctions, and significantly so after the absence of such effects in département choices, were differences between first and second home owners. Thus, second home owners were more inclined to seek a home in the open countryside and to be attracted by a property that needed restoration (although this effect is almost completely due to the greater propensity of retired and pre-1988 second home owners to seek a property to restore). On the other hand, second home owners were less attracted by large land plots and were less likely to select their home because it was 'just what they wanted' (Table 4.8). Other than these considerations, other key stimuli to home selection, including finding a 'character' property (property agents defined this as clients searching for their own 'Rose Cottage'), good local scenery, a village location, a large property and a good value purchase, all demonstrated no real differences between buyers according to the time of property purchase or the intended home use. That the main distinction between first and second home owners is linked to open countryside habitats should not lead us to assume that this is due to a greater desire amongst first home owners to integrate with local communities or for easier access to village facilities. If this interpretation was accurate, then village location and access to facilities would distinguish these two groups.

The key difference between first and second home owners relates to their different emphasis on the home as a 'sanctuary' and as a source of income. For second home owners, having a property that was away from others provides an isolation that makes the dwelling a real break from their everyday lives; as indicated by 6.3 per cent of post-1987 buyers who went beyond expressing their desire for an open countryside home to state that it had to be a property that could not be overlooked by other people (the percentage for pre-1988 buyers was only 3.8, but this was still greater than first home buyers in either period). At the same time, as an escape from the everyday, it comes as no surprise that few second home owners wanted encumbrances that could raise problems for them while at their home; hence the lesser emphasis on having a large land plot (indeed, all those who explicitly stated they wanted small land plots were post-1987 second home buyers). That a relatively high percentage of pre-1988 second home owners were looking for a property to restore is perhaps linked to the greater emphasis these buyers placed on acquiring a cheaper property (Table 4.8). Certainly, it is notable that post-1987 first home owners were more interested in property restoration than their pre-1988 equivalents, as well as being more concerned about property prices than second home owners who purchased properties at the same time. This owes much to the fact that, for first home owners, property restoration offers the potential to earn a living in France; if only because it means that a larger home can be obtained for the same money, which offers the prospect of renting part of the home to holiday makers. This prospect should be well known to potential buyers, as French property magazines regularly provide information on the income potential from a French home, of the major share that British holiday makers have in gîte rentals and of the mechanisms and requirements involved in becoming part of the national Gîtes de France chain. [4] Hence we find that 6.3 per cent of post-1987 buyers explicitly stated that what attracted them to their property was the future ability to rent part of it to others. Of course this figure, as with the privacy component in second home purchasing, is by no means a dominant effect. The dominant issues in home selection are very much aligned those of seeking a rural home, with rurality directing search behaviour, and home features more commonly distinguishing between precise dwellings. As such, differences between buyer groups over issues like property prices reflect shades of dissimilarity between buyers, little else.

This is a general point about our results. Certainly there are differences between first and second home owners, as we saw in the emphasis second home owners gave to access to Britain (Table 4.6), and in their preference for open habitat locations (Table 4.8). Yet dissimilarities between these groups is restricted to a few, often self evident issues. This is a different picture from that obtained from studies of second homes in Britain. It is true that second home owners in the UK tend to move to places that have suffered job losses and outmigration (Bielckus et al., 1972; Bollom, 1978), much as in France (Bontron and Mathieu, 1977). However, for the migration of permanent residents to France we see inflows to areas with slight potential for employment growth and hence, for those of pre-retirement age, into areas with limited work opportunities. This points to the prospect that the second home literature has less applicability to British flows to France than studies of counterurbanization (or its rural in-migration component at least). But intra-national studies of counterurbanization also do not offer much succour. For one thing, a large number of British first home owners in France are of a working age but have no job to go when they relocate. Studies of in-migration into rural areas of Britain generally provide a different picture from this, as with Dunn and associates (1981) recording that around one-third of all in-migrants to rural Herefordshire came for employment reasons (also Dean et al., 1984; Perry et al., 1986). Moreover, in British counterurbanization movements there is often a strong element of return migration (e.g. Dean et al., 1984; Jones et al., 1986), which does not apply for British moves to France. Also to be considered are links between first home inflows and the second home market, for just as higher second home owner incomes often give them greater access to housing than local residents (Bollom, 1978), so too should first home owners be able to outbid those seeking a second home because their disposable income is allocated toward just one property (this would not apply if there was a sharp difference in income between these groups, but our data on British buyer occupations indicates this is not the case). In fact, estate agents in France report that there is little direct conflict between first and second home owners over property acquisitions, although this is due to the abundance of rural properties in the areas that British people favour. But now we have come full circle, for the fact that there is a plentiful supply of cheap housing merely emphasizes the brittle nature of these local economies. For second home owners this is not a major consideration. As a part-time resident, the beauty, calm and charm of rural areas is what they want to consume. For those of retirement age exactly the same point could be made. But what of first home owners of pre-retirement age? They need to bring in the coins as well as spend them. Identifying that their geographical distribution and, in the main, their reasons for moving to France, are little different from second home owners raises interesting questions about their motives for leaving Britain and their intended lifestyle once in France. It is to the first of these considerations that we now turn.

Emigration from Britain

The first point to make clear is that the overwhelming majority of those who move their first home to France are coming from Britain. Media presentations at times refer to expatriate communities in Dordogne (in particular), in a manner which suggests that an enclave of former colonial administrators live there (whose ties with Britain as a place of habitation have been weak for some time). This is an incorrect image of the 'permanent' British population of France. Thus, among our British first home buyers, the proportion of pre-retirement age that came to France from a place other than Britain was just 9.1 per cent (and only 6.4 per cent for post-1987 migrants). The figure for those who moved at or in retirement is 21.3 per cent (18.2 per cent for those coming after 1987).

Perhaps differences in previous home location account for some temporal changes in the reasons why permanent migrants moved to France, although the factors that drew people from Britain and from elsewhere are quite similar. As Table 4.10 shows, in good measure permanent migration to France has been stimulated by disenchantment with Britain. This is explained by respondents in various ways:

West Sussex is over crowded, mainly with the wrong sort of people. (permanent resident, Calvados)

Recession in the UK drove us out - our house was repossessed and we lost everything. (permanent resident, Charente Maritime)

The general encroachment of town into country, the proximity of nuclear stations and the generally materialistic attitude of the present day UK. (permanent resident, Dordogne)

1. Dissatisfaction with career and work environment
2. High UK property values / low French property values
3. Alarm at long term effects of Thatcherism
4. Enhancing opportunities for children (permanent resident, Lot)

Thus, while the dominant cause of movement amongst pre-1988 movers was stated to be retirement, amongst later migrants disenchantment with economic, political and social change in Britain was more influential. One Lot resident who had moved permanently to France captured the flavour of many responses:

We all came here chasing some kind of dream. For some, that is fulfilled by spending a few weeks of each year in their French home, cooking cassoulets, drinking 'cahors' on their vine covered terrace as the sun goes down ...So far, so good [but] ... A large proportion seem to come to France to escape difficult work, family or financial situations in Britain. They come *from* rather than *to* and the move is seldom a complete solution.

However, we need to be aware that our statistical measures of this phenomenon do not identify its true magnitude. Thus, in mail survey responses, many informants gave the answer 'on retirement' as their reason for moving to France, in the same way that they did in household interviews. However, when interviews were conducted there was the opportunity to prompt further, with the result that many respondents indicated that it was their dissatisfaction with what was happening in Britain that led them to consider leaving the country on retirement. Yet, while not a major factor in absolute terms, the proportion of informants who indicated that their international move was stimulated by a desire to 'get away from Thatcher' was twice as high before 1988 as during or after this year. [5] Nevertheless, what the declining importance of retirement as a cause for migration identifies, is the growing importance of pre-retirement relocations. Thus, we find more people arguing that their main reasons for migrating to France were the need for a change in lifestyle, a better climate, a cheap place to live or a more relaxed mode of living.

But how do we interpret this mixture of reasons? To begin with by pointing to similarity in the importance of work related moves over time, as well as to their slight role in bringing pre-retirement migrants to France (Table 4.10). Beyond this we should ask whether comparisons over time might be affected by changes in the composition of the migrant population. After all, 63.9 per cent of post-1987 first time buyers were of pre-retirement age, compared with a figure for earlier years of just 38.2 per cent. To see whether such changes in migrant profiles were influential, Table 4.10

Table 4.10   Percentage of first home owners giving stated reasons for moving their main home to France

	All pre-1988 buyers	All post-1987 buyers	Pre-retired post-1987 buyers	Retired post-1987 buyers	All buyers in all years
Changed home on retirement	35.7	14.2	0.0	37.8	21.1
Disliked changes in Britain	16.1	22.8	23.4	20.0	21.1
Liked French lifestyle	14.3	20.5	22.1	15.6	18.4
Cheap to live in France	5.4	20.5	22.1	20.0	15.7
Employment opportunity	14.0	15.0	23.4	0.0	14.6
Needed a change in life	7.1	13.4	15.6	11.1	11.4
Wanted a better climate	3.6	11.8	9.1	17.8	9.2
Changed home on early retirement	5.4	11.0	6.5	20.0	9.2
Disliked job in Britain	8.9	3.9	6.5	0.0	5.5

Source: Authors' survey

divides post-1987 buyers into pre-retirement and post-retirement groups. Apart from self-evident differences associated with jobs or (early) retirement moves, the only notable distinction between these groups was the greater desire of retired migrants to move to an area with a better climate (see also Hoggart and Buller, 1994b). Noticeably, the proportion that explicitly stated that they were disgruntled with changes in British society was no different for retired and pre-retired households.

The level of that dissatisfaction is even more apparent when we examine the circumstances under which people would consider returning to Britain. Here we must point to a caveat in informants' answers, for frequently these were couched in terms of a move being extremely unlikely but might be considered under certain circumstances. In Table 4.11 we have leaned towards caution, so any circumstance that might lead to a return being *considered* is listed as if it could produce a return, even if strong statements were attached expressing severe doubts that this would result. Most notably, though, the often stridently expressed view that people would never return to Britain dominated our responses. Moreover, with the exception of retired households being more prepared to consider a return on the death of a partner (perhaps partly because pre-retirement householders were less likely to think of this event when answering an open-ended question), there was little to distinguish the responses of pre-retirement and post-retirement home owners.

Table 4.11   **Percentage of first home owners naming factors that might make them move back to Britain**

	All pre-1988 buyers	All post-1987 buyers	Pre-retired post-1987 buyers	Retired post-1987 buyers	All buyers in all years
Under no circumstances	54.4	41.4	41.0	44.4	45.5
Deterioration in health	15.8	9.4	6.4	11.1	11.8
Death of a partner	8.8	10.9	6.4	17.8	10.2
If family needed arose	10.5	6.3	6.4	6.7	7.5
If income prospects were better	7.0	7.8	10.3	4.4	7.5
Perhaps the unexpected	3.5	8.6	6.4	13.3	7.0
If France was politically unstable	3.5	7.8	7.7	6.7	6.4

Source: Authors' survey

We are left then with a situation in which 25.6 per cent of all British informants moved their first home to France at a pre-retirement age (with another 20.7 per cent being first home owners of retirement age). Moreover, the situation is one in which the percentage of all home owners in France that are permanent residents of pre-retirement age is on the increase (being 19.1 per cent of all pre-1988 buyers, but 26.9 per cent of post-1987 purchasers). The reasons that these pre-retirement households give for moving to France, for choosing a département and even when selecting a specific home, are not so different from second home owners. At the same time, the factors that prompt the decision to leave Britain, with a few self evident exceptions, are not distinguishable from those of retired people. Significantly, this means that the vast bulk of pre-retirement first home owners place significant weight on consumption criteria in their migration decisions.

Household finance

This clearly raises the question of how householders derive sufficient income to stay in France, given that so few go there with a job arranged or a business opportunity beckoning. Most certainly, with the exception of farmers and manual workers, few migrants retained the same occupation after their move. Of those of pre-retirement age, for instance, only eight of the 22 teachers continued in that profession after moving, with figures of four from 11 company directors and two from six business managers. Moreover, 34.0 per cent of all pre-retirement movers indicated that they had no job in France. However, on scrutiny we find that this self reported

Table 4.12   **Attributes of property rental by British owners**

	Pre-retired First home owners	Pre-retired second home owners	Retired first home owners	Retired second home owners
% renting property out	19.2	21.2	6.3	13.6
% stating they will rent in the future	5.1	1.2	0.0	0.0
% renting for 14 or more weeks	47.4	0.0	20.0	0.0
Mean average weeks rented out	13.5	6.6	10.2	6.2

Note: The '% renting for 14 or more weeks' and the 'mean average weeks of rental' are calculated only for those who did rent their property.

Source: Authors' survey

occupational standing does not reflect the reality of household income, for those who earn money from renting part of their property to holiday makers often did not count this as an occupation in France. Thus, whereas 26 of our first home owners obtained income from renting property, only four listed gîte rental as one of their jobs and two of the five who named property rental as an occupation do not rent their own home but act as agents for other people's properties.

To appreciate the importance of property as a source of British income in France, we should note the character of British property purchases, as well as the spectrum of British involvement in property related occupations. To start with, it is pertinent to provide information on the level of rental activity that is currently underway, with the caveat that some permanent residents indicated that their rental operations were not fully operational as yet, with some not having started at all; although this was the intention once property restoration or restructuring is complete. So, whereas only 8.1 per cent of pre-retirement first home respondents indicated that they had purchased their home because it had rental potential, 19.2 per cent now earned income from renting out part of their property, with a further 5.1 per cent indicating that they were determined to do so in the future (Table 4.12). Moreover, although various respondents indicated that their rental operations have not reached their full potential, many households already receive rental income for more than 14 weeks, which is the mean average rental time for gîtes in France (Warburton, 1992).

When we examine the properties that these renters buy, we find a clear pattern emerging which links future rental activity to home selection. This pattern becomes clear when we remind ourselves of the greater importance of cheaper property in the home selection decisions of first home owners, not only when selecting France (Table 4.6), but also in choosing a département (Table 4.7) and in decisions on specific homes (Table 4.8). This pattern is understandable in the context of people moving to France with no fixed job on arrival. What is clear is that many British home owners move permanently to France because they are persuaded that property rental and other property related activities are capable of providing them with a sufficient income. Moreover, a considerable number of these migrants believe that France is a cheaper country to live in than Britain (Table 4.10), so their demands for income generation are expected to be less. Selling a home in Britain, especially at a time of high house price inflation (Chapter Two), thereby provides a significant capital asset which remains as a substantial sum even after the purchase of a cheap home in France (so providing a stock of money that can yield interest to live off). Even so, if a move is to be made with the uncertainty of no job, then preserving the core of any capital earnings is an relevant consideration. Not surprising then that first home owners who rent out part of their property were more likely to regard cheap property prices as a major attraction in French home ownership (with 45.8 per cent of all first home owners who rented out property and 52.6 per cent of renters of pre-retirement age giving this as a primary reason for selecting France, compared with 28.1 per cent for first home owners who did not rent out part of their home and 39.3 per cent for those of pre-retirement age). [6]

In addition, in seeking to reduce costs, many buyers acquire properties that are in need of substantial repair, and then undertake considerable work on the home themselves. Thus, whereas only 15.4 per cent of renters had not made a major change to their property, in the form of restoring a derelict house, changing a non-residential building to residential use, building an extension or undertaking a major restructuring of the design of their home, the percentage for non-renters was 30.8. In doing this work, 80.0 per cent of renters who made home improvements did some of the work themselves, with 32.0 per cent completing all the work on their own (the percentages for first home owners who are not involved in renting out property are 58.6 and 24.1). As for the kind of changes that were made, 61.5 per cent of renters report that they upgraded a second building on their property so that it was fit for residential use (14.5 per cent for non-renters), with 30.7 per cent having to upgrade their primary home (23.2 per cent for non-renters). It is no surprise, given the derelict or non-residential character of many of their properties, to find that few renters bought a home that already had a swimming pool (3.8 per cent, with 4.4 per cent for non-renters). However, with French property magazines making clear that it is much easier (and more lucrative) to rent properties to holiday makers if homes have a swimming pool (e.g. Gilpin, 1992), it is perhaps not surprising that 15.4 per cent of renters report that they have since built one (compared with 3.8 per cent for non-renters). [7]

But holiday rentals are not the only activity that British residents are attracted to with a property flavour. For instance, eight first home owners run a chambre d'hôte or bed and breakfast operation, with a further nine stating that they were involved in property care (which ranged from cleaning swimming pools and homes, to being a gardener, to looking after second homes while their owners were not present). It is relevant to note that those involved in such activities had had a variety of other occupations in Britain. Those running chambres d'hôtes, for instance, include for a car seller, teachers, an import-export trader, an artist and a water authority executive. Those in property care were drawn from accountants, students, builders, farmers, musicians, communication technicians and journalists. What we again need to stress is that migrants would have been aware of the possibilities of working in the property care field before they left Britain, even though they might not have fixed an opening for themselves prior to departure. Thus, French estate agents hold that many British owners are not equipped for maintaining a second home in France or for living there for any length of time without regular assistance (Buller and Hoggart, 1993). As a result an extensive 'after sales' service has developed, with companies providing a variety of property services. Some of these property companies are linked to existing estate agencies (such as Maisons Dorées at St Cyprien in Dordogne) but many others are wholly independent operations. [8] In addition, when potential buyers were contemplating French property ownership, they would be aware that many British people have been employed by French estate agents to help with translation, promoting property sales in Britain and dealing with British clients when properties were being viewed. Even a cursory review of French property magazines makes this clear, as many companies include the names of their 'English' workers or state that they have British employees. [9] Moreover, it is in the property field that we find most manual workers, with carpenters, electricians, stonemasons and other construction workers accounting for the bulk of our respondents who had manual occupations in Britain. Additionally, occupational changes on moving to France were often associated with the building trade, as well as often being linked to a change from a white collar job (like teacher or artist) to manual work. At the same time, many who have set up their own business in France are involved in construction or tourism (restaurants, gîtes, hotels, chambres d'hôtes, caravan sites). [10]

The importance of this property emphasis increases when we take account of those who came to France with an arranged job. Thus, based on their work in France, approximately half of company directors, farmers, managers and teachers had a job to come to or a business opening to take up when moving to France. If we remove these from our list we find that the most important new roles for working British emigrants are renters of their own homes, manual labour, teaching the English language, craftwork, caring for property, farming, operating a chambres d'hôte or restoring or building houses. Amongst these roles, only manual labour, farming and craftwork are not associated with substantial shifts in occupation once people move to France. [11] Moreover, many of the jobs the British hold are not full-time. Thus, even including those with arranged jobs, just 57.4 per cent of British immigrants had full-time jobs, with 25.7 per cent working part-time and 16.9 per cent only working seasonally. Indeed, amongst those who did not rent out their property, 14.1 per cent of pre-retirement first home owners reported that no household member had anything other than a seasonal or a part-time job.

As we saw when examining the reasons why people are leaving Britain, a considerable proportion do so because they are disenchanted with their lifestyle in their home country and wish for a better life for themselves and their family. Illustrative of this sentiment are the views of two of our respondents:

> A desire to change life completely, give up careers and try something else in a better climate, and out of the 'rat race'. (permanent resident, Lot)

> This area of France seems to be how I remember England was, some years ago. A slower pace, less crowded, very relaxing. (second home owner, Calvados)

What rural France offers is an environment that captures (some important dimensions of) the lifestyle they seek, while being a cheap place to live. For permanent residents, it is the low cost of accommodation that offers the capital reserve to fund a lifestyle they desire (magazine articles often stress the amount of leisure time British owners have). As a further indication of this pattern, fully 39.7 per cent of pre-retirement households with no rental income indicated that they received no income in France at all (only two were unemployed at the time of our survey). [12] In a some cases this appears to have resulted from work being undertaken for British (or other non-French) firms, as with writers or contract workers. However, more commonly it came from people having sold a business in Britain (with a significant proportion of builders and company directors in this group) or else having an occupation that offers a pension at an early age (like the police force or the armed services).

Effectively, many households opt to forego improved income prospects in order to live in what they see as a superior home and environment. Exactly the same applies to those who come to France in the hope of earning an income from property rental or from picking up part-time or seasonal work or even, if chance wills, a full-time job. For many of these people sacrifices have to be made in order to achieve the lifestyle they want:

> We lived in a two man tent erected inside the property for over two years, renovating the home around us. Everyone thought we were mad. Some still do. (permanent resident, Charente Maritime)

> Most British people I have met end up being worse off financially than they expected. (permanent resident, Lot)

> Love it here. Hard to leave. Also never worked so hard for so little profit. (permanent resident, Dordogne)

> It's hard work. Don't come here with lots of romantic illusions unless you are very rich! You have to work bloody hard! (permanent resident, Charente Maritime)

With so many respondents from South East England, it is appropriate to draw attention to Fielding's (1992) ideas about the character of social mobility in this region. What is notable here is a tendency for white collar workers to 'step off' its escalator of rapid job promotion; effectively, having made more rapid social advances than their counterparts in other regions, southeastern workers often 'opt out' rather than continuing to move up the occupational ladder. Backed by rapid house price rises and the accumulated capital that house sales bring (Hamnett, 1992), it appears that rural France has become a highly desirable option for those who opt out of this southeastern escalator.

Conclusion

In our introduction to this book, we pointed to the merits of Mabogunje's (1970) systems view of migration, with its emphasis on drawing out the evolving character of linkages between sender and reception points; with the nature of these linkages stimulating or restricting the development of migration streams. What we have seen in this chapter is that such linkages do not have a strong prior base for British households who purchase French homes. Few of our respondents had lived in France before, a surprisingly small number had taken holidays there in recent times, and a great many had no ties of family or friendship with that country. Only for those who emigrated before 1988 do we find a significant family connection, and this group accounts for few of the British population (e.g. Table 4.1). What lies behind most British home purchases, then, is not an established array of formal linkages. More notably, as we found in Chapter Two and as reasons for choosing France indicate (e.g. Table 4.6), sharp increases in British house prices (particularly in the South East) had a catalytic effect on buyer activity because they made French homes appear extremely cheap. For many households this led to a realization that they could afford a second home or could escape an undesirable work or home situation in Britain. Cheap house prices offered the opportunity to acquire a rural home, without necessarily drawing people to France:

> I realize France is geographically larger than the UK for approximately the same population. This perhaps allows for the better opportunities to live in a rural environment than England if so desired. To me, France's greatest asset perhaps is the large open spaces still there, allowing for a style of life not available in England because of the number of people and lack of land available for housing at a realistic price. (permanent resident, Calvados)

> I find articles about living in France most over-rated. I would imagine it is no better nor worse than living in England, just completely different and hard to compare. (permanent resident, Charente Maritime)

In addition, of course, property price hikes provided a necessary financial base from which to fund consumption oriented purchases. The strength of this consumption orientation is then seen in a lack of distinction in the criteria that first and second home owners gave for selecting their French home; with rurality, climate, scenery, access to water and acquiring a 'picture postcard' home, all looming large in decisions. Amongst those who have permanently relocated to France, few are driven by an employment motive. Many are prepared to live off the capital they brought from England (or which is provided from there through a pension) or take the chance of obtaining jobs they are not specifically trained for and which often are not full-time. Others see their property as the major source of their future income (with some second home owners obtaining rental income to offset the costs of home purchase: Table 4.12). For second home owners, properties offer a temporary haven away from their everyday lives. But for those who have relocated their main home, a French property represents either an escape from an undesirable lifestyle or an opportunity to grasp a superior lifestyle in rural France. But with limited linkages to France, one has to ask how people developed their appreciation of the French rural lifestyle or at least saw it as superior to anything they could achieve in Britain. This issue is what we turn to in the next chapter, for our contention is that the opportunity afforded by cheap house prices and the prospect of owning an 'ideal' rural home do not by themselves explain the magnitude of British flows to France. As estate agents and media reports make clear, many of the Britons who move their main home to France have a slight prior knowledge of the French language, [13] so that undertaking a permanent home relocation is a significant step to take (at pre-retirement age especially). What is needed to encourage people to take this step is the sense that they will find their 'dream'. For this, positive feedback on the reality of living in rural France is needed from those who have already taken the plunge. How far then is living in rural France seen as being 'ideal' amongst contemporary British home owners?

Notes

1   Details of the methodology used here can be found in Hoggart and Buller (1993a). In brief, household questionnaires were used for a random selection of 'British' people/names in rural areas of Calvados and Dordogne. A mail questionnaire was used for Charente Maritime, Lot and Vaucluse, where a random selection of 'British' names was taken from telephone directories covering the whole of each département. The same questionnaire was used in both surveys.

2   The Ville de Paris is département number 75, when referring to the Paris region we include Seine et Marne (77), Yvelines (78), Essonne (91), Hauts et Seine (92), Seine Saint Denis (93), Val de Marne (94) and Val d'Oise (95).

3   With so little work on British house buying in France we were conscious of the desirability of not 'forcing' interviewee responses into a preconceived checklist. Consequently, all questions on home selection and reasons for moving to France were open-ended. This does mean that the percentages we report are likely to under-estimate the degree to which buyers considered these factors in their decisions, as open-ended questions tend to illicit only the most central factors that people consider (Moser and Kalton, 1971). What our survey responses reveal, therefore, are not absolute measures of the importance of decision criteria but an indication of their relative importance (assuming under reporting and over reporting are randomly distributed).

4   Thus, the March 1992 issue of *French Property News* contained five articles on 'making the most of your French property', with the October 1992 issue including articles on options for bed and breakfast provision and membership of Gîtes de France. The latter of these not only emphasized that grants are available for bringing properties up to required standards but also noted that one third of gîte rentals go to British nationals (Warburton, 1992).

5   This again raises the issue of how to interpret open-ended questions, for we have taken this description literally (with only 5.4 per cent of respondents stating their case in precisely these words). Examination of other reasons for leaving Britain make it clear that the economic, political and social transformations that occurred in Britain over the 1980s were disliked by many emigrants.

6   For reference, by département, renters who were first home owners of pre-retirement age were more likely to be found in Calvados (20.0 per cent), Dordogne (23.1 per cent) and Lot (29.4 per cent). Lot also stands out because its residents were easily the most likely to indicate that a primary reason for leaving Britain was that France was a cheaper place to live (29.4 per cent, followed by Charente Maritime at 23.1 per cent). Calvados and Charente Maritime stand apart because more of their residents came to France with an arranged job or business opening (33.3 per cent for Calvados and 30.8 per cent for Charente Maritime), yet a high proportion of their pre-retirement first home owners were also leaving Britain due to disenchantment with the changes it was undergoing (30.3 per cent and 30.8 per cent).The other three départements score much lower on these criteria, with a complexity of factors as reasons for leaving Britain amongst their residents. Yet Calvados and Charente Maritime are less notable when people's unwillingness to return to Britain is explored. So, while Charente Maritime is the only département in which more than half the pre-retirement emigrants claimed that they would never return to Britain (53.8 per cent), the percentage for Calvados (42.9) was little different from those for Lot (41.8), Dordogne (38.5) and Vaucluse (37.5).

7   This information was obtained from an open-ended question about the property improvements owners had made to their home. Although we received very detailed responses from many owners, we know these figures under report the presence of swimming pools. This was apparent when interviewers asked who put in a pool that was immediately in front of them, after interviews had been completed in which no mention was made about buying a home with a pool or adding one later.

8   For example, among advertisements in the January 1993 edition of *French Property News*, there are entries for swimming pools (Fox at St Amand Jartoudeix), plumbing and electrical work (Alan Simpkin of Rénovations Rurales at Maël-Carhaix), renovation (David Harbourne at Plaudren), property security (Peter Richie at Noaillan), housekeeping (Propercare at Payrac), property rental (European Connection at Dinan) and investment assistance (Jaeger Expatriate Services at Monbazillac).

9   In some instances British migrants establish their own companies in France, as with Agence NPS at Thury-Harcourt in Calvados and Denis Dodridge at Eymet in Dordogne. At other times, 'English' names appear as negotiators for French firms, as with Liz Lloyd for Immobilier Bouchet-Vaquié of Auch, Mark Dowling for Agence Klarer at La Coquille or Jill Brown, who has been listed as negotiator for each of Agence Miremont, Cabinet Jante and Immobilier Jardin. Perhaps less notable today than it was two or three years ago (largely as British sales have declined and French agents have become more confident in handling British clients and promotions on their own; Buller and Hoggart, 1993), advertisements by French estate agents commonly list 'English' contact names without specifying their precise role in the company (owner, employee, contract work, etc.).

10   Again we should point to the regularity with which French property magazines make their readers aware of these possibilities. Selecting a few instances at random, *French Property Buyer* has had articles on those who have established a hotel in France (Anon, 1991b), set up a book shop (Jeffery, 1992a), run a camp site (Jeffery, 1992b) or established a construction business (Albert, 1991; Anon, 1992a). In the last case it is notable that both articles point out that these companies operate largely by servicing British home owners; thereby suggesting that obtaining employment is not so difficult as might have been thought (articles on property management and the design and overseeing of property renovations suggest the same; e.g. Anon, 1991c). Likewise *French Property News* has carried articles for potential British migrants on farming (Paice, 1991), trout farming (Rudnick, 1991), establishing a small business (Anon, 1992b; Parkinson, 1993), running a tourist outlet, such as a chambre d'hôte, a gîte or a camp site (Warburton, 1992; Crabb, 1993a, 1993b; Street, 1993) and undertaking craftwork (Hick, 1993). However, these magazines do inform, so the potential difficulties of home purchase and relocation are not ignored. That there is a cautionary side to employment is well illustrated by a letter in the July 1991 issue of *Living France* (p.16): 'Two years after first deciding to move to France we finally arrived in September 1990. By November 1990 we were back to England! To cut a very long story short, my husband and I obtained all possible information on all aspects especially regarding my husband working for himself (self-employed) as a property and garden maintainer. When we went to the Chambre des Métiers we were told in a very painfully lengthy explanation that to become self-employed you have to pass an exam IN FRENCH in accountancy, public relations and advertising ... What makes things worse is that we've got a lovely big house with a huge garden in a lovely area. The children loved all there was to offer in France especially school and we now have to try and sell it'.

11   Teaching English as a foreign language is the most important job after property rental for all pre-retirement British migrants (second equal with farming). However, whereas all bar one of the farmers in our sample indicated that they had followed farming as an occupation prior to migrating to France, not one of the English language teachers

indicated that they had undertaken this sort of work in the past. Not surprisingly, half of the English language workers had been a teacher of some sort prior to moving to France, but the range of occupations that people had before taking on this work was extensive (e.g. incorporating those who had worked as artists, broadcasters, journalists and speech therapists).

12   Although no subdivision was made by home used, in a survey of 2,517 readers of *French Property News*, 61.3 per cent of existing owners stated that they had bought their home with a cash payment (63.8 per cent of intending purchasers indicated that they would do the same), so only 38.7 per cent of existing owners required a mortgage (Wisefile Ltd., 1992).

13   We did not ask respondents about their language ability, as we felt that answers would be extremely difficult to compare, as well as being subject to a significant 'upward drift'. Thus, although property agents informed us that the French language ability of many of their buyers was poor, it is notable that the *French Property News Survey* reports that only 11.6 per cent of those who had already purchased a French home defined their own language ability as 'non-existent', with 69.9 per cent claiming a 'passable' knowledge of French and 20.6 per cent stating that they were 'fluent' in the language (Wisefile Ltd., 1992). Summarizing the information we received, the word 'passable' is probably more accurately stated as 'basic'. In line with reports that we received in interviews with French estate agents and British agencies promoting French property sales, newspaper and magazine articles make it clear that many British buyers have a slight knowledge of French, with numerous articles identifying people who bought a home in France without being able to speak any French (Anon, 1991a; Sweeting, 1992). As a survey of agencies for *French Property Buyer* (June 1990, p.16) indicated, '... many French agents have not only recognized the surge of interest that is currently coming from Britain, but have also spotted that most buyers are far from confident in making themselves understood in anything but their native tongue. To this end ... [they] are keen to stress that they have bilingual staff' (also Buller and Hoggart, 1993).

5 Living in rural France

The literature on the integration of immigrants into reception communities indicates that adaptation is influenced by length of residence, education, knowledge of the local language and whether association with an immigrant's own group is preferred (e.g. Richmond, 1988). For the most part, British migrants to France are recent arrivals, with a relatively poor knowledge of the local language; although their social standing points to educational levels that should ease transition into new communities. Even so, theoretically, we should expect British migrants to be disadvantaged by the consumption orientation of their home acquisition, as this places them as 'pastoralists', who, compared return migrants, job searchers, commuters or retirees, face the greatest problems of acceptance by existing populations (Forsythe, 1983). This at least is the position in the abstract. On the ground we find deviations from this according to the character of receiving communities and the motivations of migrants (Richmond, 1988). As regards the receiving community, as Chapter Two outlined, we need to be conscious of prior depopulation in many of the areas that British buyers favour. Thompson (1970, p.43) captures something of the experience of these areas and in doing so offers insight on why in-migrants might be positively received by local people:

> The ultimate expression of rural depopulation is thus an aura of decay, not only in the physical sense of abandoned buildings, but in the social sense of a deprivation of services, distractions and comforts of twentieth century living.

Moreover, many of these rural areas have long experiences of recreation based inflows, as Thompson (1962) reports for the département of Isère, where depopulation gave the base for existing homes or cheap land plots to be turned into second homes for outsiders. British home buyers are doing little more than repeating this process, but often in places that have not attracted major inflows of French second home ownership (Figures 2.5 and 3.4). In addition, many British buyers seek a permanent rather than a seasonal residence. Added to which, as British buyers are drawn to the open countryside (Chapter Four), their impact on local housing markets is lessened, not simply by their desire for older properties but also because of the tradition of farmer retirement to villages (e.g. Wylie, 1974). Alongside the abandonment of farm buildings due to agricultural restructuring (Ministère de l'Agriculture, 1992), this commonly means that British buyers occupy 'unwanted' dwellings. If we also note the improvements that British owners have made to the quality of the rural housing stock (Hoggart and Buller, 1994c), then British home owners should receive a warmer reception in rural France than international migrants in many other settings; assuming that the trickle of British buyers in individual communities does not become a torrent that unbalances housing markets and social norms.

This seems unlikely, as the rural idyll that so many British buyers seek could not be sustained under the force of a British 'invasion'; at the very least this would destroy the 'authenticity' of their experience by turning their rural haven into a British tourist spot (Buller and Hoggart, 1994b). It is as well to recall that the literature already warns us of the dangers of urban in-migrants trying to live out their idealized image of rurality after coming to the countryside (e.g. Forsythe, 1980). But the prospect of British in-migrants 'capturing' the social life of their recipient communities is an unlikely scenario; for they are small in number and are operating in a foreign language (in which many are not fluent). Moreover, the slight prior knowledge of rural France that many migrants seem to possess is likely to weaken any tendency toward assertiveness that could be apparent within Britain. [1] Whatever the cause, it is clear that British purchasers expect rural French communities to live up to their 'ideal' image of a rural haven. How else can we explain the extraordinary behaviour of some buyers, as one letter to *Living France* (March 1991, p.13) clearly demonstrates:

> We purchased a house in St Pierre d'Othe (1-2 hours Le Mans) through an advert in your magazine by Office Immobilier Lavallois Bourget. Mr Alex Cameron dealt with our enquiry and without speaking one word of French (now taking lessons) we purchased a home without the problems we have experienced in England. How was this possible?
>
> Purchased your magazine pm at Smiths, Truro. Same evening saw a house we fancied. Rang home number of Mr Cameron, he assured us it was a good buy ....
>
> Next day, 9 am faxed through confirmation willing to purchase. 9.30 am rang bank to swift deposit through, so within 20 minutes of phoning we purchased a house in France. Mr Cameron arranged a mortgage and insurance. We eventually came over to settle the purchase of the house. Arrived on the overnight ferry, completed purchase the next day at 10.00 am with Mr Cameron as our interpreter.
>
> We could not believe it was possible to buy a house with so few problems. When we eventually saw the house we were delighted and got far more than we expected for £29,000 including fees.

The answer as to why British people are prepared to make snap decisions on French property is unlikely to be due solely to its cheapness, for figures like

£29,000 are hefty sums to waste. Perhaps low prices enable quick decisions to be made, but they do not cause them. Yet many buyers decide on their property almost as a whim, as the following buyer reports indicate:

> I have a lot of respect for Phil Corfield, an electrician who spoke not a word of French. On his first visit to France - his first holiday abroad ever - Phil marched into an estate agent and bought an old barn in the Dordogne. That takes a lot of courage. (Anon, 1991a)

> Buying the house was the easiest part. We weren't even looking. But when we spotted a run down little *maison a vendre* in the heart of medieval Castillon du Gard, it was hard to resist. Especially when we learned the price - £35,000 ... within two months the house was ours. (Chubb, 1991)

> I was travelling and found myself in the village of Montcuq. I saw the empty *pharmacie* and fell in love with it. The original fittings were all there, lovely oak shelves painted yellow ochre and naturally battered, what they call distressed in the antique business. I just thought how good those shelves would look with books on them and that was that. Within a few months the bookshop was open and doing business. (Jeffery, 1992a)

Cheap prices make 'dream' homes more easily attainable, but there must first be a desire to acquire such properties. At a general level, there is an abundance of evidence that British people, and especially the middle classes, are deeply attracted to the notion of rural living (e.g. Young, 1988; Thrift, 1989). But buying a home overseas, especially for those with meagre personal knowledge of the country and locality involved, and particularly when changing a primary residence, is a big step. To make this move, buyers have to be convinced that they will find the 'dream' they are in search of. In this chapter we first explore, through an examination of newspaper and magazine articles, the abundance of information that is available to potential buyers; the vast bulk of which presents a 'rosy' picture of British lives in rural France. We then examine whether these images hold good in reality and assess what this means for the integration of British home owners into French rural communities.

A welcoming vista

There are various dimensions to buying a property in France that appeal to people. At one level, there is the status that owing a foreign property bestows. Perhaps amongst buyers in the early 1980s there was also the added attraction of 'discovery'. For, unlike media coverage that later emphasized the hard work, expense and length of time it took to renovate a property (e.g. Chubb, 1991; Green, 1991; Briarty, 1992b), even during the peak years of 1988-1990 a premium was attached to finding a 'wreck' that was ripe for restoration (Hoggart and Buller, 1994c). The 'dream' of finding such a home enhances the home acquisition experience, as property dereliction increases the sense 'uniqueness', by allowing the buyer to imprint personal taste more completely on a home (Phillips, 1993). The potency of this prospect is well recognized by the advertising industry, as evinced in recent television images of a 'friendly' building society offering cash for the restoration of a 'discovered' large country home that was succumbing to nature due to its earlier abandonment. Precisely this vision is provided by innumerable accounts of how British buyers have 'discovered' their French rural home:

> The owner climbed aboard a small motorbike and took off over a rough farm track. Ruth and Michael followed in their car. Eventually they arrived at the tumbledown place. Some of it was three hundred years old, some just a hundred. But all of it was falling down. An old woman had lived there alone. When she died it had stood empty for eight years. The garden was a jungle, the roof a colander, the wooden floors were eaten away. A mess, a ruin, a wreck. Ruth and Michael decided to buy it at once. (Drew, 1991)

> We drove into the derelict courtyard of La Guyomeraie at lunchtime, and for both of us it was truly *le coup de foudre* (love at first sight) ... Grouped around three sides of a large courtyard were a tall granite L-shaped house and three stone barns. Nearly all the doorways and windows had elaborate carved mouldings, and over one door there was an indecipherable coat of arms. We waded through the nettles under the walnut trees to peer as best we could through the filth of the windows. The house had been empty for about two years. (Anon, 1990a, p.27)

> Finding lost treasures is always part of the fun of buying an old property. (Briarty, 1992a)

Of course the continued existence of properties that lie unoccupied for years is one indication that British buyers do not directly compete with French people in local housing markets.

Whatever encouragement this might give people to take the idea of French property ownership seriously is certainly intensified by reports of the warm welcome that incoming Britons receive from their new French neighbours. One example of this was provided in the November 1991 issue of *Living France* (p.34), wherein a new British home owner was startled by his neighbours reactions when his furniture was impounded by French customs:

> On our second day we had a surprise visit from our wonderful new neighbours, total strangers, who could not fail to see our serious situation. Shortly afterwards we were greeted with the awesome sight of half a house load of loaned furniture coming over the hill on strong French shoulders. Such spontaneous kindness is a constant delight to anyone new to this country.

Even worries about children who do not speak French find solace in media reports:

Elizabeth was a little worried that her children might be seen as slightly odd [at school], as the only English pupils, but they were welcomed from the start. In fact their nationality gave them a touch of celebrity. (Anon, 1992a, p.14; see also Yorke, 1993)

Beyond this reports emphasize the quality of French rural life. In this, we find particular contrasts between the French rural idyll, and both the 'grind' of living in Britain and the lack of British options to match the French experience:

After years in England of working hard just to stand still, the lifestyle here is absolutely brilliant. (Gates, 1992b)

Tim and Jayne Anderson live in central London. Two years ago, fed up with the pace of life in the fast lane, they decided to look at the possibility of buying a second home in the country. They thought of buying a cottage in the South of England, until they realized how expensive it was. They thought of buying somewhere in Scotland, until Tim .. decided that the appeal of hours driving along the M1 wasn't really what he wanted. A friend of theirs had bought a house in the Dordogne in France, and both Tim and Jayne, who are both in their thirties, were impressed at how reasonable the prices in France were. (Green, 1991)

I suppose it's a bit foolish to spend so much time in France, working in my difficult profession as an actress ... I do lose jobs. But it's so lovely I just think 'Sod it, we'll go'. (Drew, 1991, p.11)

The fresh vegetables you find in the markets - blowsy mushrooms the size of tea plates, glossy purple aubergines, fat bundles of asparagus - induce a feeling of deep despair when you recall the supermarkets at home. (Russell, 1991a)

We've converted our barns into four holiday homes and by January were fully booked for the summer. We've put in a swimming pool and we and our five year old daughter are very happy. We've been swimming since May. We often drop Laura at school and go to the beach for the day. We lived in Watford before. It took one and a half hours to commute 15 miles into London. Our cost of living is no lower here but it's lovely not having a mortgage and we are making enough to live on. (Webb, 1993)

With cheap property prices and, for those seeking a permanent move, regular magazine features offering evidence of successful employment initiatives, the scene is set for a highly idealized vision of France.

What qualifies this glossy picture are reports about the hidden costs of property purchase and the costs of home restoration. Much less commonly, articles also report problems in establishing a business in France; whether due to difficulties in obtaining a bank loan, in understanding bureaucratic regulations or in the costs of meeting high quality standards (e.g. Anon, 1991b; Horn, 1992; Jeffery, 1992b). Yet there are few reports of British

102

people experiencing social difficulties in France. Only occasionally do you find an article that points to difficulties in settling there:

> We should have thought it out before. But you can imagine how hard it was for him [their physically handicapped son], not being able to understand the language, not having all the local activities he has here [Britain], the television being all in French. We had to come back very quickly. (McGhie, 1991)

Some articles also caution against too ready an assumption that a livable income can be derived in France (e.g. Allen, 1991; Jeffery, 1992b), with most indicating that adapting to work is harder than people generally realize (e.g. Paice, 1991; Rudnick, 1991; Warburton, 1992). Yet only a cursory glance through magazine and newspaper articles indicates that their tone is generally upbeat, that the picture presented is an attractive one and that reports by buyers themselves are consistent with these sentiments.

Moreover, as studies of rural in-migrants in Britain show, often movers are prepared to accept a more uncertain and less generous income, so long as they enjoy a more relaxed lifestyle (e.g. Dean et al., 1984; Jones et al., 1986). As many such migrants are driven by a desire to escape the 'urban rat race' (Bolton and Chalkley, 1990), what France offers for British home owners is greater security in finding this new lifestyle. This was particularly evident during the late 1980s, when house price inflation in Britain meant that buyers could buy a much cheaper (and often more substantial) French home and have a significant capital resource left. If there are privations in transferring a permanent residence to France, it appears that a substantial proportion of British home buyers were well placed to respond to them. Yet, as for second home owners, no matter how good the preparation or how realistic the expectations, reality can come as something of a shock.

Experiences of French living

The first and most important point to stress about British home owner responses to living in France is their positive evaluation of their new home area. Not one of our respondents expressed regret about having purchased a property in France and very few first home residents expressed any desire to leave France. [2] Repeatedly both first and second home owners expressed joy over their experience of living in rural France:

> It is a dream we have held for some time. The reality exceeds our wildest dreams. The quality of life for us is way above the UK, where we also had a good lifestyle in a super Rutland village. (permanent resident, Vaucluse)

> Living in France for me is much better and harder than I thought before. Better meaning more gentle, friendly, welcoming than imagined. Harder meaning integration is difficult for me because of having to learn a very hard language, familiarity with the bureaucracy, etc. (permanent resident, Lot)

We came to France to live with the French. We do not seek out other British people. We have found what is for us our particular corner of paradise. Not everywhere in France would suit us - certainly not city life. (permanent resident, Lot)

With first home owners so positive about rural France, it takes little to imagine that second home owners will be similarly disposed. After all, even in the abstract we would expect that a more limited time at a French home reduces the prospect of discomfort over missing 'British things' or finding it difficult to adapt to French living patterns. In addition, as second homes are more inclined to be used for vacations, their owners are likely to be positively disposed to their French property because of its association with leisure; and if they tire of visiting the same place each year for their holidays or find less satisfaction with the area than they expected, then selling the property is likely to be less traumatic than for those who were intent on changing their permanent place of residence. Not surprisingly, therefore, second home owners are quick to reveal their pleasure over owning a French property:

We think, and so do all our family, that buying this house is the best thing we have ever done. (second home owner, Dordogne)

A superb place, I only wish I could transfer my business commitments there. No hassle, plenty of space, clean towns. I cannot praise it enough. (second home owner, Calvados)

For myself I would quite comfortably live here all the time, but financial circumstances and two young children dictate otherwise. (second home owner, Charente Maritime)

However, if we go no further than recording such positive attitudes we will not represent the depth of feeling that lie behind the views of second home owners. It is true that only 6.9 per cent of second home owners indicated that they would make France their permanent home at a later date, but there is no doubt that the attractions of French living are greater than this figure suggests: [3]

Having originally bought the property on impulse it is now my long term intention to retire to France, probably splitting my time between the existing property and another further south ... As each year passes France's virtues - its richness, uncrowded roads, high standard of living, good scenery - become more apparent. By contrast the UK (except areas of no employment possibilities) is uniformly grimy or overcrowded or both and the mentality of the population as expressed through the tabloid press is depressingly moronic. There's really no contest. (second home owner, Lot)

Living in France is for us a sheer delight. We have been considered from the start as part of the local community and we love village life. Our house is in the heart of the village and we have made good friends here. We came to France to absorb France and be absorbed by it

... We made this our second home only because of our children living in England. Had we no family we would no doubt have lived in this home permanently. (second home owner, Dordogne)

The message that this Dordogne owner gives is of some significance. The draw of rural France was bound up with visions of an 'unspoilt' countryside and a 'rustic' home; with a lack of knowledge about France and its language favouring less grandiose expectations about social integration. Yet what we find once households are installed in France is a deep sense that their new neighbours have welcomed them with open arms.

In terms of providing systematic evidence that reflects this message, the most impressive figure that we can give is that 97.6 per cent of our informants who expressed a view agreed with the statement that their French neighbours had been 'very friendly' toward them. The strength of this feeling did not vary with the date a property was purchased, by département or according to home role (e.g. Table 5.1). Moreover, it is significant that few home owners reported that their 'best friends' locally are British (Table 5.1). Given that second home owners reported a strong incidence of speaking French, of being a Francophile and of already having family or friends living in France (Table 4.6), their lesser tendency to report British friends is perhaps expected. Yet only a small minority of first home owners reported that they had British friends locally. More commonly, respondents reported that they take active steps to become part of the local French community:

Having lived in four foreign countries in nearly 20 years, I believe the most important step is 'integration' into the local society. Here French is essential but making the effort to have good relations with the villagers is more important than perfect French. Any newcomer (French or foreigner) who stands aloof doesn't stay very long. (permanent resident, Vaucluse)

One has to make an effort to integrate with the local people and to speak French however badly. For example in winter [we] have been to [the] local café to play bingo to improve number concept. Never play in England. (permanent resident, Vaucluse)

We believe the only way for full acceptance by the local French is to live like them - to speak the language and not to try to change their way of life. We join in their local committee not to dominate but to help. We have found it infinitely more rewarding to mix with the locals than with other British ex-pats. (second home owner becoming a permanent resident, Calvados)

What also has to be stressed is the emphasis our respondents gave to the ease with which they have felt part of their local community:

English friends (we do have some) are absolutely amazed when they stay with us at the friendliness of the French. I can honestly say not one French person has been rude to us in our own time here. (permanent resident, Calvados)

Table 5.1   **Percentage of British home owners agreeing with statements about living in France**

	Pre-1988 buyers		Post-1987 buyers	
	First home owners	Second home owners	First home owners	Second home owners
Best local friends are British	27.3	20.8	26.7	20.3
Neighbours very friendly	98.1	100.0	96.8	97.4
French resent British home owners	50.0	13.6	23.2	13.0
Social life quiet in winter	17.6	29.0	29.1	32.6
Public services good	77.8	83.7	82.2	86.7

Note: These percentages are calculated without including those who replied 'no view', as these were predominantly recent arrivals in France.

Source: Authors' survey

There are only four dwellings in our hamlet and all our neighbours have made us feel very welcome. Our nearest neighbours are pleased to see the house lived in again and the improvement in appearance has pleased them. (second home owner, Charente Maritime)

The French are a great deal easier to live with than British propaganda allows. If you take the trouble to learn the language - or even *try* - the people are exceptionally friendly. (permanent resident, Vaucluse)

I have found my neighbours to be friendly and helpful from the start. They were so pleased that I was not a Parisienne - they are the anathema of the French country people. (second home owner becoming a permanent resident, Calvados)

We cannot stress how well we have settled in here, due largely to the help and friendliness of all strata of local inhabitants. (permanent resident, Charente Maritime)

I just feel very much *at home* in France; enjoying it all. (second home owner, Charente Maritime)

Sentiments of this kind are representative of a general pattern of people stating that their decision to buy in France was one of the best decisions of their life. Considering that an explicit question on how British owners evaluated their decision to buy a French property was not included in our questionnaire, it is instructive that 13.9 per cent of respondents spontaneously made statements which indicated that they regarded living in France as 'superb'. Not one respondent expressed the view that they had made an error in purchasing a French home. [4] All we need add to this is to note that the propensity to make such positive comments was marginally greater for first home owners than for second home owners. [5]

It is little surprise, then, that few permanent residents wish to consider returning to Britain:

> I hope that would never happen. I have limited means and although I have had to look for part-time work recently I would rather live even more simply than move back to England. (permanent resident, Lot)

> This is not a prospect either of us wish to contemplate. We are quite content where we are. (permanent resident, Charente Maritime)

> Would *anyone* rather live in Britain than France? (second home owner, Charente Maritime)

> I find it difficult to think of circumstances that would make me move now that I am settled here. The reorganization of changing would be too much trouble. (permanent resident, Dordogne)

Stated in a more systematic fashion, 45.5 per cent of first home owners stated that they foresaw no circumstances in which they would ever return to live in Britain. This figure bore no relationship to previous experience of living abroad, as the percentage that expressed this view was 45.8 for 'ex-pats' who had not lived in Britain for some time. Moreover, it was not age dependent in a significant way, for 42.4 per cent of pre-retirement householders felt this way, with 50.6 per cent of our respondents who were retired agreeing. Although not surprising, length of residence in France did distinguish between respondent views, with 54.4 per cent of pre-1988 buyers seeing no prospect of a return to Britain, compared with 41.4 per cent of later buyers. However, if this sentiment is conditioned by length of residence, then the longer recent buyers stay in France, the greater the prospect that they will see no merit in leaving this country. Moreover, the above figures are conservative ones, for they identify those who explicitly stated that they would consider a return under no circumstances. Anyone who qualified their response was 'classified' under a different heading. Illustrative of a response that we classified as 'would consider returning' were the comments of one permanent resident who had set up a retirement home in Lot:

> Only if a health problem could not be properly dealt with locally - but most unlikely. We like it [here] and expect to die here.

Comments of this kind that were linked to health were made by 11.8 per cent of permanent residents, with the death of a partner being the second most important prompt that might lead people to consider a return to Britain (at 10.2 per cent). Equal with family reasons, the third most important consideration was the first that involved a general comparison of Britain and France. This arose over money matters, with 7.5 per cent of first home owners indicating that they would contemplate a return if this improved their standard of living:

> Should we find that we can get a much better return on our capital from a portfolio of property in the UK, as opposed to holiday lettings in France. (retired permanent resident, Dordogne)

Putting together the bundle of reasons that might draw people back to Britain (better income, lower house prices, a job, retirement, a lower crime rate) or that would make them consider leaving France (political instability, more British arrivals, health problems, the death of partner, income reductions), we find that only 16.6 per cent of permanent residents envisage any positive features of Britain that could draw them back. This compares with the 34.2 per cent who report that only deteriorations in their living circumstances in France would provoke them to contemplate a return (just 4.8 per cent gave both positive and negative reasons). Clearly few want to return to Britain. Moreover, for those who might leave France, some would not go to Britain:

> We have no desire to return to the UK and even if we had to leave or choose to leave France, it is unlikely that we would choose the UK because of the climate, crime and unrest. (permanent resident, Lot)

Integration into local communities

All this might give the appearance that British people find it easy to become part of their local French community. Such an interpretation would exaggerate reality. As various respondents report, despite the warmth of their welcome, for many there are cultural barriers to climb:

> Although I had worked with French people before we bought the house it was not until I spent time there regularly and acquired a circle of French acquaintances (mainly Parisian with second homes in the Lot) that I realized how strong were the cultural differences between the English and the French. France, despite its proximity and familiarity, seems much more 'foreign' than a number of other European countries. (second home owner, Lot)

> We accept every opportunity to get to know our French friends and neighbours better. We adopt the systems of work, taxation, health care, pensions . . . We adapt our styles of cooking, we even speak a sort of 'franglais' between ourselves. But we still hope Radio 4 stays on long wave, we like to read English newspapers and magazines and talk English amongst out compatriots. Whilst wanting to become part of the local scenery, we find it impossible to adopt a total camouflage. We will always be *les anglais du coin*. (permanent resident, Lot)

This sense of separation was evident in the messages of some second home owners. Here the tone was generally positive, but for many this was matched with an unambiguous view that France was a desirable as a second home but not as a permanent place of residence:

> Living in France, as a permanent resident, must involve an element of stepping out of English life. This may suit some but it is not for me! Undoubtedly there are advantages particularly for those who have lived abroad a lot and have therefore fewer roots. All must enjoy the chance of more sunshine, cheaper wine, greater variety of food, good restaurants, lack of social responsibility (affects some only) but the ties of family and friends must be ruptured if not broken. (second home owner, Dordogne)

> The French are very family and nation orientated, less receptive to foreigners. There is a very strong national identity and one could never integrate wholly. In short, we are happy being there for 7-12 weeks a year. No more ! (second home owner, Lot)

The point that is made by this Lot respondent is one that various informants made. It is representative of a minority of cases in which householders pointed to aspects of the local French community that inhibit social integration and adaptation to life in France:

> The French are more family orientated by tradition or religion than the English and probably less receptive to foreigners - they probably have the strongest national identity in Europe which one has to respect. One could for the above reasons and others not integrate properly in France - they are well educated, charming, have a better sense of manners than the English - in short we like being here for seven weeks maybe up to three months per year but not more. (second home owner, Lot)

> In general French people are much more reserved than English people, as a result of which they are harder to make close friends with, and therefore many of the English migrants tend to stick together. (second home owner, Calvados)

Yet respondents were much more inclined to criticize their fellow nationals over any difficulties of social integration, rather than identifying the source of any restraints arising from attitudes within the local French population.

The nature of these complaints varied but points of particular note were a weak grasp of the French language and a lack of preparedness for living in a rural area that is different from Britain:

> The problems of language are understated. We all arrive here believing that we'll be speaking fluent French within a year. Virtually no one does ... Unlike some other countries that give home to ex-pats, France is a relatively proud and self confident country. The average Frenchman is not going to brush up his English to make us feel more at home. (permanent resident, Lot)

... recently an alarming number of British people have decamped here, unable to speak French, dazzled by notions of a cheap and easy life, unprepared for day to day living and unable to exist here without the support of their compatriots. It's a common immigrant problem, I'm sure, but ... the question constantly asked by bemused locals is 'why do the English come here?'. (permanent resident, Lot)

In fact, one of the most notable features of our questionnaire responses is the alacrity with which informants criticized fellow nationals for failing to exert efforts to increase their social integration.

The basis of these criticisms was stated overwhelmingly in terms of fears about that resentment toward British residents could increase amongst the French population. The grounds for such fears were various, but most significant was a failure of in-migrants to be sympathetic toward the local French population:

We live in an area (south Luberon) where there are as yet few English speaking residents. Should, however, these numbers increase we feel there *could* perhaps be some resentment as people who move into the area are often able to purchase property that local people cannot. There is also the possibility that these 'part-time' residents make no attempt to learn the language or about local habits and therefore do not integrate. (permanent resident, Vaucluse)

You don't ask if the Brits in France can speak French. Often they can't or won't - hence the 'colonies' and English speaking 'networks' which isolate them from local history, events, and personalities, to their own detriment, and create an indifference verging on antagonism in the locals who choose either to ignore or exploit the British. (permanent resident, Vaucluse)

However, for most respondents the potential for resentment is a bigger issue than its incidence. Generally, few informants recognized animosity within their own community. Thus, just 20.2% of all respondents agreed with the statement that there was resentment amongst the local population toward British home owners. Even in the Provencal département of the Vaucluse, where the attention resulting from books by Peter Mayle (1989, 1990) might be expected to have created some friction, only 24.2% agreed with this statement. [6] Yet recognition of whether resentment exists or not is influenced by periods of residence at a French home, both within and across years. Amongst second home owners, for instance, there is little recognition of resentment (with 13.0 per cent of post-1987 buyers and 13.6 per cent of pre-1988 purchasers identifying it). This contrasts with the responses of first home owners, amongst whom 50.0 per cent of the pre-1988 buyers who answered this question felt that resentment did exist, with 22.6 per cent of later first home owners agreeing. That this temporal division is not brought about by regional differences is indicated by the strongest recognition of resentment occurring in Calvados (at 42.9 per cent amongst first home owners), where the highest proportion of our post-1987 buyers are found. It is more likely, then, that those who stay longer in France become more aware of this issue as they become more familiar with the French population.

Nevertheless, our figures reveal that British residents find their neighbours extremely friendly. Whatever resentment exists, British home owners rarely experience this in their immediate social circles. Indeed, while recognizing that these sentiments are present, many Britons gain comfort from conceptualizing such views as part of a general mistrust of 'outsiders' or at least as a diluted force compared with sentiments towards Parisians or other Europeans:

> You have the choice of accepting the French way of life or pretending that it is just another part of Britain. The British who speak only English and stick together are not appreciated ... The local people do resent other people living here but not just the British - anyone who wasn't born here ... Tourism is very much a big part of the local economy but they don't like tourists. (permanent resident, Dordogne)

> French country people dislike Parisians more than British. (second home owner, Charente Maritime)

> I think far too many Britons go to France without understanding how France works. They have scant knowledge of French history or the psychology of its people and I often feel embarrassed to be driving a British car. I do not think many are good ambassadors for Britain, but the French country people dislike Parisians more than the British, so they put up with it! (second home owner, Dordogne)

> Resentment against 'incomers' is reserved for Parisians whom the locals do not want at all. (second home owner becoming a permanent resident on retirement, Calvados)

> In our immediate area (Périgord Noir) there are very few British retirement or secondary homes, but a lot of Dutch, who started coming here massively in the '60s and '70s. The Dutch have been instrumental in arranging, and in some cases paying for, the restoration of touristic sites. No British activity in this direction so far. As to resentment against foreign home owners this is towards the more numerous Dutch than the few British. (permanent resident, Dordogne)

Most certainly, from our interviews with the mayors of communes and with other government officials, we can confirm that local rural leaders felt that British residents were either little noticed or were making real efforts to become part of the local social scene. Even so, many British respondents insist that some of their compatriots are not making genuine efforts to integrate socially. Indeed, some hold that those who cling to their own kind do not do so in response to what they find once they arrive in France. As one experienced property agent in this housing market reported, British expectations about social integration are not uniform even when buyers make initial inquiries about French home acquisition:

... buyers divide into two categories: those who prefer to live where they have been on holiday; and those who go deep into the heartland because they are desperate to escape their compatriots. (Spittles, 1992)

In a sense, the existence of groups that do not make active efforts to interact with the French population is not problematical, at least in so far as we have identified no hostility towards such people (with the significant caveat that we have undertaken no general survey of local attitudes toward incoming Britons). However, the question of scale is important, for it is possible that an enhanced British presence will bring any 'isolationist' behaviour into sharper focus (especially if increased British numbers raise competition over housing and other local resources). It also begs the question of whether British attitudes towards their fellow nationals are driven less by concern over the reactions of the French population and more by the 'threat' that extra British residents pose for the 'uniqueness' or 'genuineness' of the French rural experience. Much as middle class migrants in rural Britain are accused of being keen to close the door on other incomers after they have acquired 'their' rural dream (Cloke and Thrift, 1987; Shucksmith, 1990), perhaps these grumblings represent the early stages of opposition to inflows of 'like' people who could 'spoil' a new found 'exotic' home patch. Certainly, those British residents that do complain about the behaviour of their fellow nationals seem to have their own 'pet' theories about who is not integrating socially. To cast light on whether these assessments are accurate or perhaps represent concern about the diminution of French home ownership dreams, we now examine the main distinctions that our respondents made between British residents who are integrationist and isolationist.

Permanent residents and second home owners ?

As regards a failure to integrate socially, for those living in France permanently, the most criticized British people were second home owners:

> There are too many English people using France as their second home; not contributing to the local community, loading their cars with UK bought goods. (permanent resident, Calvados)

> We deplore the arrival of holiday home owners who do not attempt to speak the language and seek the company only of their fellow countrymen. (permanent resident, Lot)

> I tend to avoid 'second home Brits' *at all costs*. My observation of these people is that they treat their corner of France as a British colonial outpost, which does not endear them to the local people, nor does it make me terribly proud to be of the same nationality. (permanent resident, Charente Maritime)

The essential complaint here was encapsulated in the comments of a second home owner. This Charente Maritime resident expressed the underlying grievance of many British home owners using the words: 'It is a pity that some British residents do not appreciate that they are living in someone else's country and not still GB'. The grounds for this complaint were captured by the words of a Lot second home owner, who charged that: 'Far too many English colonize, rather than integrating. Why on earth do they come to France?'. That both of these summary points were made by second home owners is instructive, for while permanent British residents in France often criticize their second home counterparts, many second home owners are keen to become part of their local community. What is more, as we showed in the previous chapter, in terms of their previous experience of France, through holidays, visits to their département of home purchase and knowledge of the French language, second home owners are generally better prepared for adapting to rural France than first home owners. Moreover, many wish to be part of their new local community:

> Amongst the English we know here, the 'second homers' are generally affluent, in holiday mood and integrate well. (permanent resident, Lot)

> We are 100 per cent integrated into the local community - most years we spend all summer, Easter and Christmas/New Year here. All our friends are French; we entertain them and they us in our respective homes here and at our home in England. We do not care much for other British home owners here: they moan a lot about nothing much and are best avoided. (second home owner, Dordogne)

> We wish we had done it sooner. We came to live with the French, not the English. (second home owner, Charente Maritime)

> Too many damned British! (second home owner, Charente Maritime)

This suggests that distinctions between first and second home owners are not as notable as first home owners suggest. Indeed, in responses to a final open-ended questionnaire item, which asked if informants wished to add comments about living in France that were not covered in the questionnaire, the complex nature of first home - second home distinctions became even more apparent. At one level, for instance, 7.0 per cent of first home owners stated that other British people in their area were an 'embarrassment', with 3.2 per cent stating that too many British people lived in their area. In the nature of so open-ended a question, the small stature of these figures is to be expected, yet they are instructive in pointing to distinctions between groups. For both, second home owners recorded lower responses (at 2.4 per cent and 1.9 per cent, respectively). Moreover, 10.3 per cent of first home owners stated that they found local French people exceptionally friendly towards them, compared with 6.7 per cent of second home owners. When we check to see if such dissimilarities extend to the social activities that informants ascribed to themselves, we again find points of distinction. With little to separate those who bought their home at different points in time, only 39.5 per cent of second home owners reported that they belonged to any local organizations (cultural, educational, environmental, social or whatever), whereas the figure for first home owners was 86.7 per cent.

Table 5.2   Percentage of British home owners reporting that they purchase household goods in Britain

	Pre-1988 buyers		Post-1987 buyers	
	First home owners	Second home owners	First home owners	Second home owners
Food & other everyday buys	40.4	21.2	44.5	23.9
Electrical goods	7.0	7.7	7.8	10.7
Clothes and fabrics	21.1	9.6	23.4	9.4
Furniture	8.8	13.5	10.9	21.4
DIY materials	14.0	9.6	19.5	20.1

Source: Authors' survey

These last figures are not unexpected, given that first home owners spend more time at their French residence and so have a greater incentive to engage in such social activities. Possibly the same argument explains why first home owners were more likely to report that they participated in activities organized for British residents in their area (9.8 per cent doing so, compared with 2.4 per cent of second home owners). Yet, if we hold that living in France for a bigger share of the year should orient people towards opportunities in France more strongly, then how do we explain the fact that first home owners were more inclined to purchasing goods from Britain than second home owners? In all, just 37.8 per cent of our respondents reported no purchases of household goods in Britain. However, even amongst those who report regular purchases of food and other everyday household commodities in Britain, 62.3 per cent are first home buyers, with those who reported that they only buy specific items in Britain still being dominated by first home owners (being 75.0 per cent of all such respondents). As Table 5.2 shows, when we examine purchases of clothes and other fabrics, of DIY materials and of electrical goods, first home owners are also as likely, if not more likely, to buy commodities in Britain. Only for furniture is this pattern not present, but this might be because many first home owners do not buy furniture at all, having bought items from their British home with them when they moved to France. [7] Hence, the tendency toward permanent residents being more tightly bound to France in their economic and social actions is not unambiguous.

Moreover, we should note that when asked if any aspect of living in France had surprised them, 27.0 per cent of first home owners identified the friendliness of local people, whereas only 19.0 per cent of second home owners made this point. Given that first home owners have less prior experience of France and fewer prior links to that nation than second home owners, it seems likely that this higher figure owes more to a lack of knowledge (and expectations) than it does to differences in attitude towards the local community. Further pointing to the dubious nature of a clear distinction between first and second home owners is the lack of difference between these groups in the proportion who used our last open-ended question to emphasize the necessity of making strong efforts to integrate with the local community (4.7 per cent for first home owners and 4.4 per cent for second home owners).

Overall we have to emphasize that British home owners in France have found a warm welcome. Despite recognizing limitations on the extent to which they can 'fully' integrate with their new local communities, most respondents stressed that they are attempting to become part of the local social scene; irrespective of whether they are first home or second home dwellers. From the information at our disposal, we cannot support the criticisms that some British residents levy against second home owners. In so far as there are Britons who seek to live a socially 'isolated' or 'British enclave' existence, the membership of this 'group' does not appear to be linked directly to home usage.

Distinctions by age ?

Referring solely to first home owners, a permanent resident of Lot brought into highlight a possible explanation for this. This was achieved by pointing to the different types of British migrant who come to rural France:

> Crudely speaking there are: [1] retired or early retired who tend to integrate much more slowly and are often more jaundiced about the FRENCH, living in France not for the French, etc., etc. An extraordinary Somerset Maugham mixture of folk; [2] the mid life refugees like ourselves who make a lot of how well they have adjusted; except those who cannot manage a conversation in French and generally behave like superior beings; [3] driftwood of the UK recession - younger and much poorer than previous groups.

In so far as the last of these groups probably has social integration thrust upon them, owing to their need to gain employment, given that they have insufficient capital to establish a business of their own, they are likely to share many behavioural features of the second of these groups in terms of their social activities. So the essential division this Lot resident identifies is that of age. Taking the incidence of good friendships as an indication of integration into the local French community, we do find age differences. Thus, around one third of retired informants stated that their best local friends were British (35.9 per cent for second home owners and 32.9 per cent for first home owners), whereas the figures for pre-retirement households were 16.3 per cent and 23.2 per cent, respectively. This suggests that the distinctions noted above between first and second home owners are more likely to be a feature of age rather than of housing status (45.0 per cent of first home owners are retired compared with just 20.9 per cent for second home owners). Even if we only examine those who bought a home in France because they could speak French, age distinctions persist. Hence, 33.3 per cent of retired respondents in this group reported strong friendships with other local Britons, whereas just 17.6 per cent of pre-retirement householders did.

But while an age based explanation might be appealing, it should not be over stressed. For one, there was little difference in the propensity to engage in British centred social events (8.8 per cent for pre-retirement permanent residents, compared with 11.1 per cent for the retired). There was also little between these groups as regards membership of local organizations (61.7 per cent and 59.6 per cent, respectively, for permanent residents). At the same time, we found no difference in the stress that was placed on the necessity for integration into the local community. Moreover, age did not distinguish those who were surprised by the friendliness of local people (25.9 per cent and 27.2 per cent, respectively), nor did it separate those who complained of being embarrassed by other Britons in France (6.2 per cent and 6.1 per cent, respectively). Hence, while age might have a bearing on social integration, it is not a dominant factor that distinguishes the social activities of British people.

Divisions by other personal attributes ?

Housing status and age were not the only personal traits that our respondents 'charged' were responsible for aloofness toward local French communities. Illustrative of various 'targets' which were identified were people who came from South East England, ex-patriots and those of higher income:

> The English are much liked in Lot. Not quite so much so in parts of the Dordogne. But when one sees the behaviour of some of the Surrey type pricks then this is no great surprise. (permanent resident, Lot)

> Too many people move here and form a sort of English ghetto only having English friends considering themselves as ex-pats together. (semi-permanent resident, Dordogne)

> From French colleagues and friends we hear a lot about 'les anglais' in the Normandy area and in the Dordogne who *refuse* to learn or speak French, and who bring in *British* workmen to renovate their houses, when France has very many skilled artisans *still*. These attributes cause a great deal of resentment. It probably happens in Provence too, but happily there are less of these (*Daily Telegraph* readers!) about. (semi-permanent resident, Vaucluse)

Examination of questionnaire responses show that these divisions also do not go far in distinguishing between the behaviour of British residents. Thus, if we contrast first home owners from the South East of England with those from elsewhere in Britain, we find percentages of 29.5 and 25.0, respectively, for those reporting strong British friendships locally, 10.1 and 11.3 for those who participate in British centred social events, 62.5 and 68.8 for those who have joined local organizations, 28.8 and 26.2 for those who were surprised by the warmth of their reception in France and 8.8 and 1.3

for those who stressed the necessity for social integration into that community.

If those who left the UK a long time ago are taken as 'ex-pats', we again find few differences, with any dissimilarities that exist contradicting respondent statements. Thus, only 11.1 per cent of 'ex-pat' first home owners had strong friendships with local Britons (compared with 26.8 per cent for other permanent residents), 57.9 per cent had joined a local organization (60.1 per cent), 5.3 per cent took part in British centred events (10.2 per cent), while 10.5 per cent argued that social integration into the local community was essential (5.4 per cent).

Assessing whether behaviour varies across social class groups might seem beyond our reach, given that most of our respondents were from middle class occupations when working in Britain. However, criticisms that were directed at those *Daily Telegraph* readers were made by those of middle class occupation; indicating that our respondents were aware that the middle class is not a unitary social strata (Savage et al., 1992). Yet, when we compare the responses of those from different occupation groups, behavioural differences are not very apparent. For instance, when we contrast households containing teachers and those containing company directors (our two largest occupation groups), 19.6 per cent of the former report local British friends, while 20.7 per cent of the latter do. Likewise, 3.8 per cent of teachers and 6.1 per cent of company directors argued that local social integration was a necessity for British people living in France. Taking households with at least one teacher but no other member from a higher income occupation (like company directors, company managers or professionals) and placing these alongside households with company directors but no one that falls in a lower occupational bracket (like farmers, labourers, artisans and teachers in schools or further education), produces very similar results. Thus, amongst first home owners, 7.1 per cent of such teacher households were participants in British centred events, compared with 8.3 per cent of company director households. Strong friendships were held with other local British residents by 19.2 per cent of teacher households, compared with 18.1 per cent for households of company director standing , with membership of local organizations being the sole attribute that points even to a minor separation between these two groups (at 78.6 and 66.7 per cent, respectively).

Intruders in a 'dream'

None of this points to 'objective' household attributes distinguishing patterns of social integration. Yet there is no doubt that some British people are antagonized by the arrival of their fellow nationals. Indeed, for some it is disquieting to find so many British people in rural France:

> It isn't until you have bought a property that you realize how many English have bought locally. We weren't in a tourist area and particularly did not want to be surrounded by English. (permanent resident, Calvados)

In some of their comments, respondents reveal characteristic NIMBY attitudes, in that having established themselves in France they now happy about the arrival of further British families:

> A perfect antidote to London life, but please do not encourage too many Brits or Dutch to come. (second home owners, Lot)

> I hope not too many more 'Brits' come here; some who do are not a particularly good advertisement! (permanent resident, Charente Maritime)

> The French should impose an embargo on people from foreign countries in areas of concentration like Dordogne. (permanent resident, Dordogne)

Yet, as these statements reveal, such sentiments are often expressed tamely. Perhaps a reason for this is the sense of space that characterizes rural France. In 11.8 per cent of our questionnaire responses, for instance, informants made unprovoked statements about the positive qualities that low population density and open landscapes give to French rural space. Yet, some respondents felt 'their' space was under threat:

> The whole atmosphere of this part of France has changed in the 20 years we have owned a cottage here. In a village of 120 inhabitants, there were many ruined houses and an ageing population. We were one of three English families who restored village houses. Now there are English, Dutch, Danes, Irish, Scots and Germans and the character has changed. (second home owner, Dordogne)

> The French countryside still has a greater feel of 'space' than in most of the UK. Although there is much 'suburbanization' taking place with newly built (mainly French retirement - holiday) homes with 'tame' gardens, fences, etc. I am greatly concerned for this area that if a change in character of this type progresses too far it may lose much of its appeal (permanent resident, Dordogne)

Where such threats arise from non-French sources, a solution might be found in a home relocation, as one respondent explained:

> I am bilingual and worked for 10 years in French West Africa ... When I retired in 1979 we had already bought a cottage in the Dordogne where we lived until 1988. We then moved over here because the British invasion became too massive there. (permanent resident, Lot)

However, while adopting the 'exit' option creates few ripples, the same cannot be said for those who exercise 'voice' (Hirschman, 1970). There is no doubt that, for some French people, the arrival of British nationals, with their developed concerns for amenity, the environment and heritage, is a positive feature of the British presence in rural France. In Brittany, for example, the architectural pressure group *Tiez Breiz* has welcomed the actions of British home buyers in restoring old farm houses (Rueff, 1990) and much of the popular resistance to the TGV railway link through Provence was organized by a British resident of that area (Moynihan, 1990).

However, behind this latter event lies much that is at the heart of British concerns about their fellow nationals. It is one thing to arrive in France and adapt to the norms of a local community. It is another to arrive with a baggage of predispositions that could conflict with prevailing norms. This point undoubtedly underscores expressed concerns about the failure of British incomers to integrate socially with their host French communities. Put simply, if British home owners stand apart from their French communities they run the risk of failing to understand local customs and practices, with the result that tension and resentment might develop over British in-migrants. Already, for instance, certain British residents view some of the customs and practices of rural France as questionable or even objectionable:

> Dear Sir, I am writing to register my horror and disgust at one of the Small Ads in the October Issue of *The News*. This concerns a M. Veroul who 'has available fine horsemeat for human consumption'. I am sure that decent-minded people living in the Dordogne region, especially English people, would, like me, abhor the fact that horsemeat is eaten, let alone advertised. (letter to *The News* [Eymet, Dordogne], December 1991)

Even more notably, there is clearly potential for tension between British newcomers and local residents over hunting, and British respondents did complain about other activities, such clay pigeon shooting and motorbike scrambling. These objections reveal a lack of knowledge of French rural society. Hunting, for instance, is a traditional community activity, that unites people from a spectrum of social strata, through membership of hunting clubs (Weber, 1982). The chances of potential conflict are furthered because British newcomers seem unaware of the rights and traditions of *chasseurs*, which include access to certain properties and the use of frequently unmarked rights of way. In effect, the failure to develop an understanding of social behaviour in the local community often means that British residents 'confront' a local custom with an ethical argument. As interviews with local mayors revealed, this results in little sympathy being afforded to English sensibilities, with hunting often being cited as the issue over which genuine integration between British newcomers and local populations ceases. It follows that those who express concern over the behaviour of their fellow nationals, and particularly over the prospect of self contained communities, are expressing a genuine concern over the potential for future conflict.

But we must emphasize that the issue at the heart of this debate does appear to be one for the future. In our respondents' comments, we find an articulated fear that British citizens who do not integrate with the local community might eventually seek to impose their values on the local French community; one outcome of which could be the build up of resentment towards the British. What lies behind this view is the fear that an increased number of British residents will multiply the chances that such tensions will arise. At the same time, there is no doubt that, for a few British residents, what criticisms are levelled at other British home owners owes much to a sense that 'their' French dream is being spoilt as the inflow of more fellow nationals lessens the 'uniqueness' of their new home environment. That neither of these sentiments is strongly expressed at this time is hardly surprising. As Chapter Two showed, there is still a plentiful supply of old housing in most parts of rural France, so British residents still receive a warm welcome from local populations on account of the extra income they bring into the community (as well as the social merit they bestow on it because of the high value they place on a rural home acquisition). As yet, neither local housing markets nor other local services are being stretched or threatened by these British inflows. If anything they are benefiting from British buyer interest. Moreover, apart from a few areas of France (such as parts of Dordogne), the British population is too small to cast doubt over the 'genuineness' of rural France for most British incomers. [8] Particularly with low population densities, it follows that for much of rural France a substantial increase in British inhabitants will be required before residential densities reach 'threatening' levels (or even reach the level of Dordogne). Although property agents currently report that there is again increased British home buying in France, the magnitude of such sales is still too small to represent a real 'threat' to the 'exotic' nature of French rural property ownership.

Conclusion

At this point in time, the messages that home owners feed back to Britain are largely positive. It is true that there are a few media reports of distress, as with those occasioned by family bereavement, where difficulties in reselling a property can cause some trauma (e.g. McGhie, 1991). It is also the case that misunderstanding legal or other regulations has created problems for some British families. However, mainstream reactions to home ownership in France are extremely positive, with the overwhelming majority of British residents reporting that they receive a very friendly welcome from their neighbours and that the warmth of this reception has persisted over the course of their stay in France. Little resentment towards the British is identified. In fact, the French population appears to be much less critical of British residents than do their fellow British nationals. In part, the former owes something to the economic and social credit that British home buyers bring to their reception communities. On an economic front, this arises not simply from increases in the income base of the locality, through expenditure on housing and its improvement (Hoggart and Buller, 1994c), but is added to by household spending and by the creation of new enterprises. Even if gîtes and chambres d'hôtes dominate these enterprises, they still draw others visitors who spend money in the local area. Socially, gains also accrue from helping maintain the population base, and so public and private services, in areas that have often had a long history of population decline (Chapter Two).

In the context of 1980s discussions about NIMBYism in Britain, it might be tempting to see British 'antagonism' towards their fellow nationals as pique over other Britons intruding on 'personal dreams'. Yet many respondents indicated that they knew of few other Britons in their locality.

Moreover, when we examine the characteristics that respondents ascribe to those Britons who are accused of not integrating socially, no systematic differences exist across the categories that British residents themselves use. This is not to say that some British residents do not live in fairly 'enclosed' groups with their fellow nationals, with fairly limited interaction with the local French population; for there is evidence of this (Buller and Hoggart, 1994b). However, we suspect that the inability of British residents to identify how people are distinguished according to their propensity to be 'integrationist' or 'isolationist' arises for two reasons. One the one hand, it seems likely that most residents live sufficiently far away from other British residents or, with a few exceptions (such as limited areas of high population concentration and participants in British organized social events), meet other British citizens comparatively rarely, so the population base on which they draw their inferences is small and militates against accurate generalization. Even in Dordogne, our interviewers found that the distances separating British owned properties were extensive and, as the last Chapter showed, many British homes were selected for their isolation. On the other hand, it is likely that, not knowing a wide selection of other British residents, many holiday makers are assumed to be (primarily second) home owners. Whatever the case, it is clear that British residents are fearful that their growing numbers will create resentment amongst French country dwellers. Whether the political postures of Le Pen have added to these fears we cannot say, although those first home owners who indicated that they might consider returning to Britain if France became politically unstable, often explicitly mentioned Le Pen.

Notes

1   An illustration of the slight knowledge that property agents identified was uninformed views on the geography of France. Quite often places at different ends of the country were assumed to be next to one another, although the more common problem was not realizing that areas in the same region of France are far apart. As one agent described: 'Only that morning a client had suggested seeing some properties in the Gers in the morning and some in Hérault in Languedoc later on the same day, not appreciating, perhaps, that there is a four hour car journey between the two places' (Schrader, 1992). However, a poor knowledge of France is demonstrated on a much broader front than its geography. One illustration is given by the person who wrote to *Living France* (July 1991, p.17) to ask: 'Do our electrical goods used in the UK work in France?'.

2   Obviously we cannot extend this comment to those who refused to participate in our survey or those who had moved on from their former French home. However, we should point out that we had just 51 direct refusals to participate (which was 6.3 per cent of our sample after we had eliminated those we could identify as 'invalid' entries - perhaps because they were not British, had sold their former home or had died). Assuming that phone disconnections are accurate indications of households that have left or sold a former home (which we were able to

confirm in Calvados and Dordogne, where interviewers were able to ask other local residents), our estimate is that 91 'British' owners had left the French home at which we tried to contact them. Of these we traced five, of whom only one had returned to Britain (the other four moved elsewhere in France). As letters to the British media make clear, even amongst those who feel they have to return to the UK, many do so only with deep regret (see footnote [9] in Chapter Four)

3   We have to point out that this percentage is a self expressed measure, since no question was specifically asked about whether second home owners intended to convert their second home into a permanent residence at a later date. The closest we came to obtaining such information was to ask whether a home had been bought specifically with a view to retiring to it. In response to this, 15.2 per cent of pre-retirement second home owners stated that this was their intention, while a further 20.7% stated that this was a strong possibility. No specific question was included on changes in housing status from a second to main home prior to retirement.

4   We must qualify this statement with the same cautionary note we presented as footnote [2].

5   For instance, the percentages for first home owners are 17.5 for pre-1988 buyers, 17.2 for their post-1987 counterparts, 17.2 for pre-retirement buyers and 16.0 for retired first home owners. The equivalent numbers for second home owners are 15.4, 9.4, 12.0 and 6.8.

6   We make this statement with a number of considerations in mind. For one, Mayle's books have given this area increased prominence amongst British home buyers: '"British people want to buy houses in an area they've heard of", explains one specialist agent. "And because of *A Year in Provence* and *Toujours Provence* they've heard of the Luberon, even if they haven't been there"' (Anon, 1993, p.16). In addition, French property magazines do identify criticisms of Mayle by other British residents in Provence, who believe that he has brought too many British 'settlers' into the region (Laing, 1992). That the Mayle books have induced some sensitivity amongst the British in Vaucluse is evident from the odd terse statements that punctuated our questionnaire returns. The permanent resident who wrote simply, 'Don't believe Peter Mayle', represents one strand of this. Hinting at a patronizing tone in Mayle's work, which could induce resentment towards British people, a second home owner felt moved to write: 'In spite of Peter Mayle, the local people are NOT unintelligent. They are friendly, hospitable, kind and honest'.

7   There are two points we wish to make here. Both relate to possible under reporting in the figures we obtained in our survey. The first concerns the level of purchases that second home owners make from Britain, which seems low, and might be affected by respondents not recording minor items, whereas first home owners take more notice of any purchase made outside France. We expect that some element of this is occurring, but we do not feel that it is of major importance. As made clear by those who provided spontaneous comments about the quality and variety of French food, for many second home owners one of the joys of owning a French home is to get away from 'things British' and

engage in a quite different style of living for a limited period of time. The second issue concerns potential under reporting of furniture and electrical purchases in Britain by first home owners. Articles in French property magazines make it clear that many people do take all their furniture with them to France (some getting into trouble with customs over VAT regulations, others making reports on the trials, tribulations and excitement of having their furniture shipped to another country). Although, almost certainly, much of this shipped material was bought in Britain, since arriving in France many first home owners appear not to have added to their furniture stock by buying from Britain. Hence, while second home owners might buy the odd item to take to France (and so record this as a UK purchase), first home owners are more likely to have taken all their furniture with them (but, not having bought this specifically to move to France, record no furniture buys in Britain).

8   In response to an open-ended question that asked if respondents took part on British organized social activities, 9.1 per cent of first home owners indicated that they did not know of any (this answer was not suggested in the questionnaire, so the true figure for this response will certainly include some of the 81.2 per cent who simply answered that they did not). Significantly, when we compare responses by region, only 4.3 per cent of Dordogne residents indicated that they did not know of any such activities, compared with 17.2 per cent in Charente Maritime and 14.3 per cent in Calvados. For comparison, the figures for these départements for second home owners were 2.7 per cent, 12.1 per cent and 13.2 per cent, respectively.

6 Achieving the rural 'idyll'?

In this book we have sought to throw light upon the current movement of British nationals to rural France. To date, research on this topic has attracted considerable media attention but remarkably little scientific investigation. In fact, our own efforts in this domain were prompted by a growing awareness, while undertaking unrelated field research in Brittany, of the strength of French media interest in this *envahissement britannique*. Although a small number of official reports have subsequently appeared, for the most part they have focused their attention upon the specific economic and infrastructural implications of incoming, property owning Britons (e.g. Direction Régionale de l'Equipement de Basse Normandie, 1989). The press, meanwhile, has been more equivocal in its treatment of the issue; referring to *le rush anglais* (Anon, 1988), the new 'British bridgehead' (Rueff, 1990) and 'foreigners who buy up our land' (Douroux, 1989). The suggestion, which is often heard in debates on immigration to France, is that the 'threshold of tolerance' might soon be reached (Simonnot, 1991). Yet we have come across only two incidents of violent opposition to this boom. These were a campaign of spray-painted 'Brittany is not for sale' messages and the breaking of notaires' windows in the Breton département of Côtes d'Armor in November 1989. These actions were dismissed by one of the affected notaires, who maintained that British purchases of French rural property were '... not a question of an invasion but of giving back life to old stones' (quoted in Bertho, 1989). As another journalist later remarked, if France is being bought up, it is because it is being sold (Gardère, 1991). While the growing presence of British nationals in rural France is generating some reaction, this appears predominantly to be a local one. Yet even this reaction is less about the British as newcomers or foreigners than about the British as owners of French property. Thus, the images evoked are not those of a demographic Armageddon, of job losses to foreigners or of profound socio-cultural conflicts, which the Far Right commonly ascribes to such immigrant groups as the northern Africans. Rather it is of the approbation of French rural heritage, of the loss of agricultural land and of the impact on rural house prices. It was partly to assess the validity of these images that the current research was initiated. Three particular aspects of British inflow have interested us from the outset. These are: first, the role of

Britons as international migrants; second, the social and cultural consequences of British installation in rural France; and, third, the rural developmental implications of British purchases of French property. In this final chapter, we return to these three inter-linked aspects and relate them to the fundamental research questions posed at the start of this book; why France and why rural France?

International migrants: falling between theories

In Chapter One, we identified certain limitations in international migration theory in explaining population flows that are not accounted for by production led movement, return migration or refugee displacements. We further highlighted the persistent and ultimately frustrating separation of writings on international and intra-national migration. The findings documented in this book clearly suggest that the application of mainstream international migration theory to the essentially consumption led behaviour of British movers to rural France will not offer a satisfactory explanation of migrant actions. Yet explanations that hitherto have been presented to account for intra-national migration can be usefully applied to this international population movement (and possibly might apply more generally for certain flows between advanced economies). Our argument therefore is that consumption led migration across international boundaries might be better explained as a geographical extension of domestic migration processes; with that extension being prompted by the difficulty of attaining a specific consumption goal from an intra-national move, so a potential intra-national move is replaced with an international one.

The vast bulk of British movers that we studied have not sought direct productive roles within the local French economy. Very few permanent home relocations have been explicitly job-led and, while a slightly larger number have sought a living in some service capacity (such as teaching English as a foreign language or turning part of their property into a gîte or chambre d'hôte), these represent a small minority when compared with second home owners and permanent movers who derive no income from work in France. Furthermore, those Britons that earn a living in rural France do not reveal any marked distinctions in their locational choices or in their criteria for selecting France or a particular locality within it. Indeed, from our interviews with British nationals in France, there is a suggestion that some British immigrants only seek employment once their capital begins runs out (this capital often being derived from the difference in price from the sale of a British house and the acquisition of a French one). Thus, even for those engaged in the productive sector, this engagement is frequent secondary to dominant residential concerns. Furthermore, a substantial number of Britons have sought permanent residence in France essentially upon retirement. Hence, Chapter Four points directly to consumption led motivations for crossing the Channel; with climate, amenity, love of the French way of life and, crucially, advantageous property prices, dominating the decision criteria for the selection of France as a home location. It is the attractiveness of France as a residential location, and not as a working location, that brings most British property buyers to this nation and to individual locations within

125

it. Two further differences between British migrants and others have been revealed in this study. First, in contrast with the traditional picture painted for international migrants to advanced economies, British migrants to France are relatively wealthy middle class people engaged for the most part in service occupations. As we have pointed out in Chapter One, this is not enough to justify a 'rejection' of international migration theory. Nevertheless, British middle class migrants to France are demonstrably not searching for employment opportunities but seek an attractive residential location. Second, as Chapter Three has shown, their geographical target areas within France are substantially different from those of other migrants. The importance of rural areas, particularly those of western France (Figure 3.4), distinguishes Britons from the principal immigrant populations in France, as well as from other northern European nationals.

Collectively, these various characteristics reinforce our belief that standard explanations of the geography of international migration and of the choices made by international migrants are inadequate when applied to British moves to France. In short, there is a need for more consumption oriented explanations of international migration. To a certain degree, these have been supplied up to now by work on retirement and holiday migration and we have identified close parallels between parts of this literature and the patterns observed in this book. An emphasis upon quality of life and amenity in locational choices comes close to the British experience in France, as does the increasingly rural focus of retirement and vacation home migration. Nevertheless, these two literatures only offer a partial explanation for British relocations. For example, in the existing literature, the geographical choices of retirement migrants are frequently linked to personal attachments to specific locations by the presence of kin, previous residence, place of birth or prior holiday visits (Warnes, 1986; Longino, 1992). These links are manifestly less important for British migrants to France. A large number of these had not visited the region in which they bought their property before they searched for a home, while few had ties of kith and kin in the region (or even in France). Yet, despite this, Britons have been very selective in where they buy a home and have been reluctant to consider a wide range of alternative départements to the one finally chosen.

If British moves to rural France do not fit conveniently into models of international migration, might they be better explained by models more commonly ascribed to intra-national moves, such as counterurbanization? It is tempting to suggest that what we are witnessing is an extension of the counterurbanization field of urban Britain, albeit across a national boundary. This would imply that the fact that Britons have moved from their home nation is ultimately irrelevant. What is more important is that they are going to cheap, accessible rural areas, where the quality of life is regarded as an improvement on a previous place of residence. At one level, this does explain the choice of France over other European nations. There is in that country an abundance of attractive rural properties at low prices in areas of low population density. The choice of France over and above Britain as a counterurbanization destination is explained by the same characteristics. As one respondent put it:

I do not find living in Normandy very different from any extremely rural situation in the UK. The main difference is in house prices. (permanent resident, Calvados)

As we have shown, the abundance and accessibility of French rural properties, which became particularly evident to Britons at the end of the 1980s when British house prices were at their apogee, gave many people the opportunity or incentive to purchase a second home. Commonly, for these same households, this would have been out of the question in Britain due to the cost of housing.

Yet the attraction of property price differences and attractive undeveloped landscapes only offer a partial explanation of the rate and extent of recent British moves. To justify our argument, and indeed the title of our book, we need to go further in our our search for explanations of this phenomenon. After all, counterurbanization is more than a simple search for cheap properties in rural areas. It implies also recognition of a desire for an alternative, less urban lifestyle. Furthermore, a move to rural France suggests that, on top of these 'classic' counterurbanization drives, Britons are actively searching for something that cannot be found in contemporary rural Britain. At this point it is pertinent to distinguish second home owners and owners of permanent homes in France. Whereas the superficial attractiveness and the 'pull' of rural France might be the same for all, there are clear differences in the importance of French home acquisition within the residential choices of these two groups. Buying a second home with minimal amenities for £10,000 in Hérault, and spending six weeks a year there, is not the same as moving lock, stock and barrel to this département. At one level, second home owners in France are probably little different from second home buyers in Britain. Amenity, environment and the attractiveness of the locality and property are central to their house buying decision (e.g. Bielckus et al., 1972; Bollom, 1978). Property price makes an important contribution largely in so far as it determines whether a purchase is possible. Perhaps for many, what distinguishes Britain from France as a second home location is the price of a property (Anon, 1990c; Demaldent, 1990). First home buyers display a more complex set of motivations. That they have selected rural areas over urban ones is evident. However, in leaving Britain permanently, they have sought some aspect of rural life that goes beyond low cost properties. This implies that they are seeking something that they believe is now unobtainable in their home country.

France as Britain's lost rurality

French rural property ownership is becoming incorporated into the cultural experience of middle class British nationals. Even for those who do not own a French home, contemporary fiction, television and store catalogues increasingly allude to living in France. What is central to this cultural experience is the somewhat paradoxical combination of 'otherness' yet familiarity that the French rural landscape and French rural society provides.

We have already remarked upon the spatial coincidence of bocage landscapes and the most sought after départements. The bocage landscape is a familiar one for Britons, and is characteristic of both lowland and upland regions of France. Its presence over much of western France provides a convenient reference point for in-migrants, as the author Ian McEwan (1992, p.138) observed:

> Dusty tracks, unmarked on the best of maps, wind across expanses of heather, gorse and box. Deserted farms and hamlets sit in hollows of surprising greenness where small pastures are divided by ancient dry-stone walls and the paths between them, flanked by tall blackberry bushes, wild roses and oaks, have an English intimacy. But these soon give way to emptiness again.

However, in Britain such landscapes are frequently threatened by urban growth and agricultural modernization and have subsequently become highly protected enclaves of an increasingly precious rurality. Yet in France they are the landscape norm and their aesthetic attractions are largely undervalued and underused as a result. This juxtaposition of 'English intimacy', which in Britain has traditionally been managed, with a more pragmatic and less immediately aesthetic French notion of the rural landscape, is highly attractive to Britons. The relative absence of development pressures in the areas most sought by British buyers, itself a function of low population densities and the essentially periurban nature of French counterurbanization, has meant that Britons can buy with little fear of urban encroachment.

In so far as the rural landscape is both familiar (in its visual components) and alien (in its scale and its relative freedom from development pressures), it represents an idealized rural form that has no effective counterpart in Britain. It is an historic landscape that remains productive but has experienced less widescale agricultural modernization. It is populated without being urbanized. Within this idealization, there is a close parallel with notions of the British rural landscape that were common before and immediately after the Second World War (Buller and Lowe, 1991).

The cultural experience of French property ownership extends far beyond the search for an idealized and nostalgic rural landscape. As this study has shown, Britons have been attracted by an equally idealized rural way of life, the principal components of which appear to be the maintenance of traditional values, the existence of viable and genuinely welcoming rural communities, a slower 'pace of life', and an enhanced 'quality of life'. Here too, we find a strong sense of nostalgia for something that has been lost from rural Britain:

> The French attempts to preserve traditional values helps to maintain a civilized lifestyle which is fast disappearing in England. (second home owner, Dordogne)

A number of interviewees claimed that France reminded them of rural Britain of the 1950s or even before that, at which time, they maintained, a sense of rural community and local identity still existed. In France, their acceptance by local inhabitants and, where they seek it, their ready integration into commune life, are contrasted with experiences of moving into British rural communities. The presence of weekly markets where local produce is sold, the ubiquity of *boulangeries* and *cafés*, even in the smallest villages, and the multiplicity of restaurants, many of which depend upon local rather than tourist custom, remain essential parts of this rural idyll. Clearly, many of these characteristics are particular to France and their attractiveness cannot simply be ascribed to nostalgia. Nonetheless, they give a particular flavour to an idealized, yet quintessentially common rural experience, which has now effectively disappeared from Britain. We do not seek to deny the unique characteristics of France. Many of its attractions have no parallel in Britain, yet they are often difficult to define precisely. Even so, there does appear to be a general view that the lifestyle in rural France is less stressed and more enjoyable than that which is considered the norm in Britain:

> The lifestyle in this area appears to be a lot more relaxed than we are used to in Kent, people have time to chat, give one another a hand, etc. (second home owner, Dordogne).

In this context, France has come to represent the rurality that Britain is increasingly unable to provide; a rurality that is at one and the same time both an alternative to the contemporary British experience and a throwback to an idealized rural past. Furthermore, the rural dream is an essentially middle class consumption oriented one, in that it is founded upon aesthetic and non-productive notions of the role of rural space. Here, Britons moving to rural France bring with them a cultural notion of rurality that is very different from that held by the majority of existing residents (Buller and Hoggart, 1994b). Born in the nineteenth century and still dominant today, the British preservationist conception of countryside as a crucial aesthetic and a natural framework for certain types of managed human activity, is largely alien to the lived-in and worked-in *paysages* of rural France. Nonetheless, this conception finds an ideal expression in the highly attractive, yet little occupied, extensive spaces of rural France.

Clearly, the arrival of an increasing British population, occupying a social status hitherto little represented in the majority of popular host regions, and accompanied by a set of beliefs and attitudes concerning the countryside that have little to do with local practices, lends one to suppose that conflict between locals and newcomers might occur. That such conflict has not yet emerged is in large part due to the fact that Britons are generally purchasing properties in relatively isolated areas that are not sought after by local people. Furthermore, on the whole, they have shown themselves to be sensitive integrators. Undoubtedly, the boom period of the late 1980s initially attracted some speculative and short-term property buyers (Buller and Hoggart, 1994a). Often markedly less welcomed by local people, who saw them as profiteers, and existing British residents, for whom they were often an embarrassment, this group is reported to have largely disappeared as a significant purchasing group. Thus, while surveys in 1988 and 1989 revealed that 53 per cent of recent British buyers envisaged selling their property after six years (Cellule Economique de Bretagne, 1990), respondents to our survey are noticeably more committed to their French lifestyle.

Buying a home in France is like marriage - not too difficult to achieve but hard to break (second home owner, Dordogne)

I could go on about Black Wednesday and the 20 per cent decrease in my pension as a result of devaluation but I won't. I live well, obviously not prosperously, have made some good friends and acquaintances amongst the French and am very happy. Obviously I LIKE IT HERE! (permanent resident, Lot)

As for the key to understanding the acceptance of Britons, this perhaps lies in their contribution to the economic regeneration of rural areas. Yet herein lies a central and by no means uncommon paradox. On the one hand, underlying the professed attributes of contemporary rural France is a sense that any change will be detrimental to the sustainability of the sought after rural idyll. On the other hand, the warm welcome experienced by so many Britons is in part a reflexion of local people's belief that the arrival of a new population will reinvigorate the local economy. To what extent, then, are Britons the willing or unintended agents of rural development?

Reconstructing rural France

The place of Britons within the broader processes of rural economic restructuring in France is difficult to assess. Many of the most commonly targeted regions of British in-migration, particularly in the south west of France, are continually classified as amongst France's poorest; having a persistently fragile economic potential, low population densities and an inexorable outmigration of the working population (SEGESA, 1993). These are predominantly agricultural regions with little immediate possibility of large-scale economic diversification. Although many depressed agricultural regions in Europe have been revitalized by the establishment of new populations and economic activities (Fielding, 1982), the enduring fragility of much of western France suggests that employment based counterurbanization processes will have little impact. Those rural areas that find themselves lying beyond the geographical limits of acceptable industrial deconcentration require alternative paths towards economic regeneration (Limouzin, 1980). It is here that Britons are beginning to play a role, not necessarily by their own economic activities but by participating in the stimulation of a new rural vocation.

Our research has identified many examples of British initiated enterprises emerging from the 1988-1990 boom, largely in house sales and lets, estate agency in general, building and commercial operations and other service activities. Nonetheless, these exist essentially to service other British nationals. (It is worth noting in passing that the dominant observation of those involved in these activities is that dependence upon a wholly British clientele will provide only short-term economic security.) Yet, as the previous chapter showed, the presence of this new population, often in areas blighted by long-term outmigration, service closure and declining tax bases, has an obvious feedback effect upon the local economy. Not only are Britons obliged to pay land and property taxes, both on second and permanent homes, but they voluntarily make use of local services and shops. Indeed, for many this is part of the attraction of French life. Furthermore, through the employment of French labour, for construction work or for property maintenance, Britons are contributing to local economic survival. What the incoming British population is not doing, is providing an economic or demographic framework for economic investment and diversification. Indeed, this would be an anathema to most. We are not witnessing a counterurbanization process where positive migration rates and socio-demographic change accompany economic diversification and rural renaissance (Kayser, 1989). Indeed, in France, this model has arguably only a limited validity. Neither are we seeing the taking-over and challenging of traditional activities and organizations that has been the experience of intranational moves within rural Britain (Forsythe, 1980). Rather, we are observing a more subtle and culturally oriented reconstruction of the function of rural areas as we shift from occupational and productive uses of rural space to more residential and consumption oriented roles. This reconstruction process is founded upon a notion of rural space which, though largely alien to that held by the local population, nonetheless sits easily within the socio-cultural framework of small agricultural communities. The continued existence of these agrarian communities is a vital part of this reconstruction, for they are a key element in idealizations of rural life; even though their position has shifted from being the dominant user of rural space to becoming just one component of an increasingly residential environment. Britons are not the sole actors in this process of revitalization, but they are important agents of change. Not only are they the dominant in-migrant group in many rural areas, but their attitudes towards the countryside and residential amenity are well developed. Indeed, precisely these attitudes brought them to France. The process of reconstruction thus includes a transfer of values from rural Britain to rural France, which, in its own way, is a form of appropriation. Amongst Britons, this does at times become manifest in an expressed NIMBYism, which is often largely incomprehensible to the resident French population (Buller and Hoggart, 1994b). Even Peter Mayle, who has done more than most to popularize French property ownership, had misgivings about the British purchasing boom: 'I have a terrible feeling that the French would love it all. It's the refugees who hope that Provence will stay the way they found it' (Mayle, 1989, preface to the paperback edition). This transfer of values is apparent in British concerns for amenity and environment, even if these are at times alien to local preoccupations. However, given the relative availability of rural properties and the lack of alternative development trajectories in reception areas, it seems inevitable that many of the remoter areas of rural France will succumb to this genteel and partial appropriation. While individual Britons wait with trepidation to see who has bought the house next door, the French are more likely to see this inward movement as a future vocation for their remoter rural areas.

Bibliography

Albert, T. (1991) Getting on with the neighbours, *French Property Buyer*, October, 30-31

Allen, K. (1991) Time for business, *French Property Buyer*, April, 16

Alphandery, P., Bitoun, P. and Dupont, Y. (1989) *Les Champs du Départ*, La Découverte, Paris

Amar, M. and Milza, P. (1990) *L'immigration en France au XXe Siècle*, Armand Colin, Paris

Anon (1988) Le Rush Anglais, *Ouest France*, 11 August

Anon (1990a) We came, we saw, we offered, *French Property Buyer*, December, 26-29

Anon (1990b) More maison for fewer Francs, *French Property Buyer*, December, 36-37

Anon (1990c) La ruée des britanniques sur les petites maisons bretonnes, *Le Télégramme*, 11 April

Anon (1991a) A place in the sun, *French Property Buyer*, October, 22

Anon (1991b) Working in France, *French Property Buyer*, June, 15-16

Anon (1991c) Designs on France, *French Property Buyer*, December, 22-23

Anon (1992a) Cordon bleu schooling, *French Property Buyer*, August, 14-15

Anon (1992b) Le business in France, *French Property News*, September, 10-11

Anon (1993) A Thaw in Provence, *French Property Buyer*, January, 6-17

Bages, R. and Puech, J-L. (1993) L'étranger, un nouvel acteur du marché foncier local: le cas du Tarn, in Association des Ruralistes Français, *L'Etranger à la Campagne*, Nantes

Balán, J. (1992) The role of migration policies and social networks in the development of a migration system in the southern cone, in M.M. Kritz, L.L. Lim and H. Zlotnik (eds.) *International Migration Systems*, Clarendon, Oxford, 115-130

Banque de France (annual) *Balance de Paiments de la France: Annex - Origine Géographique des Investissements Directs des Non-Résidents dans le Secteur Privé Non-Bancaire (net)*, Paris

Barbichon, G. (1973) Appropriation urbaine du milieu rural à des fins de loisirs, *Etudes Rurales*, 49/50, 95-105

Barlow, J. and Savage, M. (1991) Housing the workers in Mrs Thatcher's utopia, in J. Allen and C. Hamnett (eds.) *Housing and Labour Markets*, Unwin Hyman, London, 237-253

Barnes, L.R. (1991) Field days in France, *The Guardian*, 1 June, 35

Barou, J. (1993) Les paradoxes d'intégration, *Ethnologie Française*, 23, 169-177

Bauer, G. and Roux, J. (1976) *La Rurbanisation ou la Ville Eparpillée*, Seuil, Paris

Bedford, R. (1992) International migration in the South Pacific region, in M.M. Kritz, L.L. Lim and H. Zlotnik (eds.) *International Migration Systems*, Clarendon, Oxford, 41-62

Bel Adell, C. (1989) Extranjeros en España, *Papeles de Geografía*, 15, 21-32

Belliard, J-C. and Boyer, J-C. (1983) Les nouveaux ruraux en Ile de France, *Annales de Géographie*, 512, 433-451

Bernede, S. (1989) La Nouvelle Angleterre, c'est chez nous, *La Depêche*, 12 April, 6

Berger, M. and Fruit, J. (1980) Rurbanisation et analyse des espaces périurbains, *Espace Géographique*, 9, 303-313

Bertho, H. (1989) La Bretagne n'est pas à vendre, *Ouest France*, 6 November, 9

Béteille, R. (1981) *La France du Vide*, Litec, Paris

Béteille, R. (1992) La valorisation touristique de l'espace rural, *Information Géographique*, 56(5), 210-216

Bielckus, C.L., Rogers, A.W. and Wibberley, G.P. (1972) *Second Homes in England and Wales*, Wye College Studies in Rural Land Use 11, Ashford

Bodiguel, M. (1986) *Le Rural en Question*, l'Harmattan, Paris

Boisvert, C.C. (1987) Working class Portuguese families in a French provincial town, in H.C. Buechler and J-M. Buechler (eds.) *Migrants in Europe*, Greenwood, Westport, 61-76

Bollom, C. (1978) *Attitudes and Second Homes in Rural Wales*, University of Wales Press, Cardiff

Bolton, N. and Chalkley, B. (1990) The rural population turnaround: a case study of north Devon, *Journal of Rural Studies*, 6, 29-43

Bonnain, R. and Sautter, G. (1970) Société d'ici, société d'ailleurs, *Etudes Rurales*, 74, 23-50

Bonneau, M. (1978) Le Fait Touristique dans la France de l'Ouest. Thèse d'Etat, Université de Rennes

Bontron, J-C. (1989) Equipement et cadre de vie, in A. Brun (ed.) *La Grand Atlas de la France Rurale*, de Monza, Paris, 88-92

Bontron, J-C. (1993) La reprise démographique confirmée, in B. Kayser (ed.) *Naissance des Nouvelles Campagnes*, Editions de l'Aube, Paris, 23-36

Bontron, J-C and Mathieu, N. (1977) *La France des Faibles Densités,* SEGESA, Paris

Boussard, I. (1990) French political science and rural problems, in P.D. Lowe and M. Bodiguel (eds.) *Rural Studies in Britain and France*, Belhaven, London, 269-298

Brassloff, W. (1993) Employment and unemployment in Spain and Portugal, *Journal of the Association for Contemporary Iberian Studies*, 6(1), 2-24

Briarty, C. (1992a) Normandy landing, *The Guardian*, 9 May, 38

Briarty, C. (1992b) Dreams and drains, *The Guardian*, 1 August, 34

Brier, M. (1970) *Les Résidences Secondaires*, Dunot, Paris

Brun, A. (1993) Territoires et bassins de vie, in B. Kayser (ed.) *Naissance des Nouvelles Campagnes*, Editions de l'Aube, Paris, 51-64

Brunet, P. (1992) *L'Atlas des Paysages Ruraux de France*, de Monza, Paris

Buechler, J-M. (1987) A review - guest, intruder, settler, ethnic minority, or citizen, in H.C. Buechler and J-M. Buechler (eds.) *Migrants in Europe*, Greenwood Press, Westport, 283-304

Buller, H. (1991) Le processus de counterurbanisation en Grande Bretagne et la périurbanisation en France, *Economie Rurale*, 202/203, 40-43

Buller, H. (1993) The French planning system, in House of Commons Committee on Welsh Affairs (Third Report), *Rural Housing Volume Two*, HMSO, London, 217-227

Buller, H. and Hoggart, K. (1993) French Estate Agents and House Sales to British Nationals. King's College London Department of Geography Occasional Paper 36

Buller, H. and Hoggart, K. (1994a) Vers une campagne européenne: les britanniques en France rurale, *Espace Géographique*, forthcoming

Buller, H. and Hoggart, K. (1994b) Social integration of British home owners into French rural communities, *Journal of Rural Studies*, forthcoming

Buller, H. and Lowe, P.D. (1991) Rural development in post-war Britain and France, in P.D. Lowe and M. Bodiguel (eds.) *Rural Studies in Britain and France*, Belhaven, London, 21-36

Byron, M. (1993) The Housing Question: Caribbean Migrants and the British Housing Market. University of Oxford School of Geography Research Paper 49

Campani, G., Catani, M. and Palidda, S. (1987) Italian immigrant associations in France, in J. Rex, D. Joly and C. Wilpert (eds.) *Immigrant Associations in Europe*, Gower, Aldershot, 166-200

Catanzano, J. (1987) Retour vers l'arrière pays, migrations en Languedoc-Roussillon, *Cahiers de l'Economie Méridionale*, 9, 35-43

Cazes, G. (1987) La géographie du tourisme: réflexion sur les objectifs et les pratiques en France, *Annales de Géographie*, 537, 595-600

Cazorla Pérez, J. (1989) *Retorno del Sur*, Oficina de Coordinación de Asistencia Emigrantes Retornados, Cadiz

Cellule Economique de Bretagne (1990) *Les Achats de Biens Immobiliers par les Etrangers en Bretagne en 1988 et 1989*, Rennes

Champion, A.G. (1989, ed.) *Counterurbanization: The Changing Pace and Nature of Population Deconcentration*, Edward Arnold, London

Charrier, J-B. (1988) *Villes et Campagnes*, Masson, Paris

Christine, M. (1990) La géographie des vacances, in *Données Sociales*, INSEE, Paris, 226-232

Chubb, A. (1991) When a year in Provence is not nearly long enough, *Daily Express*, 21 August, 33

Clark, R.L. and Wolf, D.A. (1992) Proximity to children and elderly migration, in A. Rogers (ed.) *Elderly Migration and Population Redistribution*, Belhaven, London, 77-96

Clark, W.A.V. (1986) *Human Migration*, Sage, London

Cloke, P.J. and Thrift, N.J. (1987) Intra-class conflict in rural areas, *Journal of Rural Studies*, 3, 321-334

Clout, H.D. (1977) Résidences secondaires in France, in J.T. Coppock (ed.) *Second Homes: Curse or Blessing?*, Pergamon, Oxford, 47-62

Courgeau, D. and Lelievre, E. (1989) *Analyse Démographique des Biographies*, Institut National d'Etudes Démographiques, Paris

Crabb, S. (1993a) Pursuing leisure for a living, *French Property News*, January, 9

Crabb, S. (1993b) Setting up a campsite in France, *French Property News*, November, 6

Crédit Agricole (1991) Mortgage à la Française: Purchasing a French Property. publicity document. Crédit Agricole, London

Cribier, F. (1973) Les résidences secondaires des citadins dans les campagnes françaises, *Etudes Rurales*, 49/50, 181-204

Cribier, F. (1979) Des parisiens se retirent en province, *Gérontologie et Société*, 3, 18-69

Cribier, F. (1980) A European assessment of aged migration, *Research on Aging*, 2, 255-270

Cribier, F. (1982) Aspects of retired migration from Paris, in A.M. Warnes (ed.) *Geographical Perspectives on the Elderly*, Wiley, Chichester, 111-137

Cribier, F. (1993) *La Fonction d'Accueil des Retraités Citadins en Milieu Rural et son Evolution Probable*, Université de Paris VII CNRS Equipe de Géographie Sociale et Gérontologie, Paris

Cross, D.F.W. (1990) *Counterurbanization in England and Wales*, Avebury, Aldershot

Crouch, D. (1992) Popular culture and what we make of the rural, *Journal of Rural Studies*, 8, 229-240

David, J. et al. (1980) *Problématiques et Méthodes d'Analyse de la Rurbanisation*, Université de Grenoble Press, Grenoble

de Warren, L. and Nollet, C. (1990) *Setting Up in France*, Merehurst, London

Dean, K., Shaw, D.P., Brown, B.J.H., Perry, R.W. and Thorneycroft, W.T. (1984) Counterurbanisation and the characteristics of persons migrating to West Cornwall, *Geoforum*, 15, 177-190

Defrenne, M. (1990) Verbal participation in the colloque, in *Partenariat avec les Britanniques dans le Bâtiment*, Direction Régionale de l'Equipement de Basse Normandie, Caen, 50-51

Demaldent, F.(1990) Verbal participation in the colloque, in *Partenariat avec les Britanniques dans le Bâtiment*, Direction Régionale de l'Equipement de Basse Normandie, Caen, 64-67

Department of the Environment (1988) *English Housing Condition Survey 1986*, HMSO, London

Dion, R. (1981) *Essai sur la Formation du Paysage Rural Français*, Durier, Paris

Direction Régionale de l'Equipement de Basse Normandie (1989) *L'investissement Britannique dans l'Immobilier notamment l'Immobilier de Loisirs en Basse Normandie*, Caen

Direction Régionale de l'Equipement de Basse Normandie (1992) *Les Proprietaires Britanniques en Basse Normandie*, Caen

Dourlens, P. and Vidal-Naquet, V. (1980) *Campagnes à Vendre*, Faculté des Sciences Economiques University of Aix Marseille II, Aix en Provence

Douroux, O. (1989) Ces étrangers qui achètent nos terres, *Pelerin Magazine*, 7 July, 7

Drew, E. (1991) The impossible dream, *French Property Buyer*, June, 10-11

Dunn, M.C. (1979) Patterns of Population Change and Movement in Herefordshire 1951-1971. unpublished PhD thesis, Department of Geography, University of Birmingham

Dunn, M.C., Rawson, M. and Rogers, A. (1981) *Rural Housing: Competition and Choice*, Allen and Unwin, London

Elliot, G. (1992) Bordering on perfection, *Daily Express*, 29 July, 39

Elson, M. (1986) *Green Belts*, Heineman, London

Faur, J-P. (1991) *Plus Loin de la Ville*, INSEE Première 119, Paris

Festy, P. (1993) Les populations issues de l'immigration étrangère, in *La France et sa Population*, Cahiers Français 259, Documentation Française, Paris, 38-44

Fielding, A.J. (1982) Counterurbanisation in Western Europe, *Progress in Planning*, 17, 1-52

Fielding, A.J. (1992) Migration and social mobility: South East England as an escalator region, *Regional Studies*, 26, 1-15

Fielding, A.J. (1993) Mass migration and economic restructuring, in R.L. King (ed.) *Mass Migrations in Europe*, Belhaven, London, 7-18

Findlay, A.M. and Gould, W.T.S. (1987) Skilled International Migration: A Research Agenda. University of Liverpool Paper in Human Geography 24

Fontaine, Maître (1990) Verbal participation in the colloque, in *Partenariat avec les Britanniques dans le Bâtiment,* Direction Régionale de l'Equipement de Basse Normandie, Caen, 52-53

Forrest, R. and Murie, A. (1990) Moving strategies among home owners, in J.H. Johnson and J. Salt (eds.) *Labour Migration*, David Fulton, London, 191-209

Forsythe, D.E. (1980) Urban incomers and rural change, *Sociologia Ruralis*, 20, 287-305

Forsythe, D.E. (1983) Planning Implications of Urban - Rural Migration. Gloucester College of Arts and Technology Paper in Local and Rural Planning 21

Frybes, P. (1992) La France, in D. Lapeyronne (ed.) *Immigrés en Europe: Politiques Locales d'Intégration*, Notes et Etudes Documentaires 4952,Documentation Française, Paris, 45-57

Gardère, M. (1991) La France à vendre, *L'Evenement du Jeudi*, 25 April, 5

Gates, J. (1992a) Channel your cash into a little piece of France, *Daily Express*, 1 April, 40

Gates, J. (1992b) Go south to the sun to beat the recession, *Daily Express*, 5 August, 33

Genet, P. (1988) Les étrangers se paient la France, *Le Point (Economie)*, 843, 129-136

George, P. (1986a) *L'Immigration en France*, Colin, Paris.

George, P. (1986b) Les étrangers en France: étude géographique, *Annales de Géographie*, 529, 273-300

Gervais, M., Jollivet, M. and Tavernier, Y. (1977) *Depuis 1914: Histoire de la France Rurale* , Volume Four, Seuil, Paris

Gilpin, C. (1992) Make the most of your French home, *French Property News*, March, 17

Green, J. (1991) Pretty as a picture, *French Property Buyer*, April, 38-41

Grundy, E. (1987) Retirement migration and its components in England and Wales, *Ageing and Society*, 7, 57-82

Gurak, D.T. and F. Caces (1992) Migration networks and the shaping of migrations systems, in M.M. Kritz, L.L. Lim and H. Zlotnik (eds.) *International Migration Systems*, Clarendon, Oxford, 150-176

Guyotat, R. (1992) De la terre aux silos, *Le Monde des Débats*, November, 5

Hamnett, C. (1992) House-price differentials, housing wealth and migration, in A.G. Champion and A.J. Fielding (eds.) *Migration Processes and Patterns Volume One*, Belhaven, London, 55-64

Hamnett, C., Harmer, M. and Williams, P. (1989) *Housing Inheritance: A National Survey of its Scale and Impact*, Housing Research Foundation, Amersham

Harnois, J. (1992) *La Localisation des Etrangers en France*, INSEE Première 177, Paris

Hervieu, B. (1993) *Les Champs du Futur*, Bourin, Paris

Hick, W. (1993) The self-employed craftsperson in France, *French Property News*, February, 13

Hirschman, A.O. (1970) *Exit, Voice and Loyalty*, Harvard University Press, Cambridge

Hoggart, K. (1990) Let's do away with rural, *Journal of Rural Studies*, 6, 245-257

Hoggart, K. (1993) House construction in nonmetropolitan districts: economy, politics and rurality, *Regional Studies*, 27, 651-664

Hoggart, K. and Buller, H. (1992a) Selling France: British Companies that Promote House Purchases in France. King's College London Department of Geography Occasional Paper 34

Hoggart, K. and Buller, H. (1992b) Selling France: Advertising French Houses to Attract British Purchasers. King's College London Department of Geography Occasional Paper 35

Hoggart, K. and Buller, H. (1993a) British Home Owners in Rural France: Property Selection and Characteristics. King's College London Department of Geography Occasional Paper 40

Hoggart, K. and Buller, H. (1993b) Estate agents, British buyers and rural regeneration in France, in E.C.A. Bolsius, G. Clark and J.G. Groenendijk (eds.) *The Retreat: Rural Land-use and European Agriculture*, Nederlandse Geografische Studies 172, Amsterdam, 96-107

Hoggart, K. and Buller, H. (1994a) Property agents as gatekeepers in British house purchases in rural France. revision of a paper given at the Anglo-Dutch Rural Geography Conference, Lancaster, September 1992

Hoggart, K. and Buller, H. (1994b) British retirement migration to France. revision of a paper given at the Franco-British Rural Geography Conference, Exeter, September 1993

Hoggart, K. and Buller, H. (1994c) British home owners and rural housing change in France. revision of a paper given at the Institute of British Geographers Annual Conference, Nottingham, January 1994

Horn, S. (1992) My kind of day, *Radio Times*, 8-14 August, 90

INSEE (1982) *Récensement Général de la Population*, Institut National de la Statistique et des Etudes Economiques, Paris

INSEE (1984) *Données Sociales*, Institut National de la Statistique et des Etudes Economiques, Paris

INSEE (1988) *Villes et Campagnes*, Institut National de la Statistique et des Etudes Economiques, Paris

INSEE (1991a) *Recensement de la Population de 1990: Evolutions Démographiques*, Institut National de la Statistique et des Etudes Economiques, Paris

INSEE (1991b) *Recensement de la Population de 1990: Logement - Population - Emploi*, Institut National de la Statistique et des Etudes Economiques, Paris

INSEE (1991c) *Recensement de la Population de 1990: Population - Activités - Ménages*, Institut National de la Statistique et des Etudes Economiques, Paris

INSEE (1992) *Recensement de la Population de 1990: Nationalités*, Institut National de la Statistique et des Etudes Economiques, INSEE Resultats 21, Paris

INSEE (1993) *Les Agriculteurs*, Institut National de la Statistique et des Etudes Economiques, Paris

Jacquot, M. (1992) La Loi du Marché, *Le Monde des Débats*, November, 2-3

Jeffery, F. (1992a) Sophie in wonderland, *French Property Buyer*, February, 13

Jeffery, F. (1992b) The other side of paradise, *French Property Buyer*, June, 31

Jones, E. (1991) Race and ethnicity in London, in K. Hoggart and D.R. Green (eds.) *London: A New Metropolitan Geography*, Edward Arnold, London, 176-190

Jones, H., Caird, J.B., Berry, W. and Dewhurst, J. (1986) Peripheral counter-urbanization: findings from an integration of census and survey data in northern Scotland, *Regional Studies*, 20, 15-26

Karn, V. (1977) *Retiring to the Seaside*, Routledge, London

Kalaora, B. and Brun, A. (1985) *Les Résidences Secondaires and l'Evolution du Tissu Rural*, Ministère de l'Agriculture, Paris

Kayser, B. (1989) *La Rennaissance Rurale*, Colin, Paris

Kayser, B. (1993, ed.) *Naissance des Nouvelles Campagnes*, Editions de l'Aube, Paris

Keith, W.J. (1974) *The Rural Tradition*, University of Toronto Press, Toronto

King, R.L. and Rybaczuk, C. (1993) Southern Europe and the international division of labour: from emigration to immigration, in R.L. King (ed.)

The New Geography of European Migrations, Belhaven, London, 175-206

King, R.L., Mortimer, J., Strachan, A. and Trono, A. (1985) Return migration and rural economic change: a south Italian case study, in R. Hudson and J.R. Lewis (eds.) *Uneven Development in Southern Europe*, Methuen, London, 101-122

Klatzmann, J. (1978) *L'Agriculture Française*, Seuil, Paris

Kritz, M.M. and Zlotnik, H. (1992) Global interactions: migration systems, processes and policies, in M.M. Kritz, L.L. Lim and H. Zlotnik (eds.) *International Migration Systems*, Clarendon, Oxford, 1-16

Labat, J-C. (1992) *La Population Etrangère par Nationalité*, INSEE Première 217, Paris

Laborie, J-P. (1993) Les petites villes, in B. Kayser (ed.) *Naissance des Nouvelles Campagnes*, Editions de l'Aube, Paris, 37-50

Laing, R. (1992) French living without tears, *French Property Buyer*, February, 16-17

Lash, S. and Urry, J. (1987) *The End of Organized Capitalism*, Polity, Cambridge

Le Bras, H. (1993) *La Planête au Village*, Editions de l'Aube, Paris

Le Bras, H. and Todd, E. (1981) *L'invention de la France*, Seuil, Paris

Lenfant, C. and Seyer, N. (1980) Résidences de loisirs: la fin du 'boom', *Moniteur des Travaux Publics*, Juillet, 18-28

Leroux, P. (1968) *Les Résidences Secondaires des Français en Juin 1967*, INSEE Etudes et Conjoncture 5, Paris

Lettre, J. (1990) Verbal participation in the colloque, in *Partenariat avec les Britanniques dans le Bâtiment*, Direction Régionale de l'Equipement de Basse Normandie, Caen, 54-56

Levesque, R. (1993) Elements sur les achats d'espace ruraux par les étrangers, in Association des Ruralistes Français, *L'Etranger à la Campagne*, Nantes

Lévy, M. and Garson, J-P. (1991) *Cent ans d'Immigration: Etrangers d'Hier, Français d'Aujourd'hui*, Institut National d'Etudes Démographiques, Paris

Lewis, G.J. and Sherwood, K.B. (1991) Unravelling the counter-urbanization process in lowland Britain, *Cambria*, 16, 58-77

Limousin, A. (1988) L'histoire de l'immigration en France: une histoire impossible, *Pouvoirs*, 47, 5-22

Limouzin, P. (1980) Les facteurs redynamisme des communes rurales françaises, *Annales de Géographie*, 495, 547-587

Longino, C.F. (1992) The forest and the trees: micro-level considerations in the study of geographic mobility in old age, in A. Rogers (ed.) *Elderly Migration and Population Redistribution*, Belhaven, London, 23-34

Lowe, P.D. and Bodiguel, M. (1990, eds.) *Rural Studies in Britain and France*, Belhaven, London

Lowe, P.D. and Buller, H. (1990) The historical and cultural contexts, in P.D. Lowe and M. Bodiguel (eds) *Rural Studies in Britain and France*, Belhaven, London, 3-20

Lowe, P.D., Cox, G., MacEwen, M., O'Riordan, T. and Winter, M. (1986) *Countryside Conflicts*, Gower, Aldershot

Mabogunje, A.L. (1970) Systems approach to a theory of rural-urban migration, *Geographical Analysis*, 2, 1-18

McEwan, I. (1992) *Black Dogs*, Picador, London

McGhie, C. (1991) Empty dreams in foreign lands, *Independent on Sunday*, 29 March, 58

McHugh, K.E. (1990) Seasonal migration as a substitute for, or precursor to, permanent migration, *Research on Aging*, 12, 229-245

Marié, M. and Viard, M. (1977) *La Campagne Inventée*, Actes Sud, Arles

Mayle, P. (1989) *A Year in Provence*, Hamish Hamilton, London

Mayle, P. (1990) *Toujours Provence*, Hamish Hamilton, London

Mendras, H. (1967) *La Fin des Paysans*, Actes Sud, Arles

Michelet, C. (1975) *J'ai choisi la Terre*, Laffont, Paris

Ministère de l'Agriculture (1992) *Graph Agri 1992*, Paris

Ministère de l'Interieur (1991) unpublished statistics of *carte de séjour* holders by nationality and département, 1980 and 1991, Paris

Mirloup, P. (1977) Résidences secondaires et finances communales, *Norois*, 94, 165-177

Moser, C.A. and Kalton, G. (1971) *Survey Methods in Social Investigation*, Heinemann, London

Mottin, J. (1992) *Les Immigrés et l'Emploi*, Librairies Techniques, Paris

Moynihan, J. (1990) Provence defends itself against high-speed train, *The European Weekend*, 25 May, 3

Muller, P., Gerbaux, F. and Faure, A. (1989) *Les Entrepreneurs Ruraux*, l'Harmattan, Paris

Noin, D. (1984) La population de la France au début des années 1980, *Annales de Géographie*, 517, 290-302

Noin, D. (1991) *La Population de la France*, Masson, Paris

OECD (1992) *Trends in International Migration*, Organization for Economic Cooperation and Development, Paris

Ogden, P.E. (1989) International migration in the nineteenth and twentieth centuries, in P.E. Ogden and P.E. White (eds.) *Migrants in Modern France*, Unwin Hyman, London, 34-59

Paice, C. (1991) Pastures new: the prospects for farming in France, *French Property News*, November, 12

Paillat, P. (1986) *Vieillissement ou Vieillesse*, Presses Universitaires de France, Paris

Paniagua Mazorra, A. (1991) Migración de noreuropeos retirados a España: el caso británico, *Revista Española de Geriatria y Gerontologia*, 26, 255-266

Papademetriou, D.G. (1988) International migration in North America and Western Europe, in R.T. Appleyard (ed.) *International Migration Today Volume One*, UNESCO, Paris, 311-379

Parkinson, C. (1993) Setting up a small business in France, *French Property News*, January, 8

Parr, J.B. (1966) Outmigration and the depressed rural area problem, *Land Economics*, 42, 149-159

Peach, C. (1968) *West Indian Migration to Britain: A Social Geography*, Oxford University Press, Oxford

Perry, R., Dean, K. and Brown, B. (1986) *Counterurbanisation*, Geo Books, Norwich

Phillips, M. (1993) Rural gentrification and the processes of class colonisation, *Journal of Rural Studies*, 9, 123-140

Plender, R. (1988) *International Migration Law*, revised second edition, Martinus Nijhoff, Dordecht

Rees, P.H. (1992) Elderly migration and population redistribution in the United Kingdom, in A. Rogers (ed.) *Elderly Migration and Population Redistribution*, Belhaven, London, 203-225

Renucci, J. (1990) Tourisme international et tourisme national dans les Etats de l'Europe meridionale, *Annales de Géographie*, 551, 21-50

Richmond, A.H. (1988) Socio-cultural adaptation and conflict in immigrant receiving countries, in C. Stahl (ed.) *International Migration Today Volume Two*, UNESCO, Paris, 109-124

Rodríguez Martínez, F. (1991) Conocimiento geograficos de la 'politica de costas' en el litoral surmediterraneo Andaluz, in F. Fourneau and M. Marchhena (eds.) *Ordenacion y Desarrollo del Turismo en España y en Francia*, Ministerio de Obras Públicas y Transportes, Madrid, 53-59

Rudnick, G. (1991) Trout farming in France, *French Property News*, November, 13

Rueff, J. (1990) Les britanniques débarquent en Bretagne, *Le Monde*, 4 April, 8

Russell, R. (1991a) Pantiles of opportunity, *[London] Evening Standard*, 9 October, 44

Russell, R. (1991b) Putting the Brit into Brittany, *[London] Evening Standard*, 27 November, 49

SAFER (1992) Le Marché foncier en 1991, *SAFER 93*, 14-16

SAFER de Basse Normandie (1991) *Les Acquisitions Etrangères dans le Milieu Rural Bas-Normand*, Société d'Aménagement Foncier et d'Etablissement Rural de Basse Normandie, Caen

SCAFR (1993a) *Les Achats Fonciers des Non Agriculteurs*, Report to DATAR, Société Centrale d'Aménagement Foncier Rural, Paris

SCAFR (1993b) *Le Marché des Terres Agricoles en 1992*, Société Centrale d'Aménagement Foncier Rural, Paris

SEGESA (1993) *Essai de Typologie Socio-économique des Cantons Français*, DATAR, Paris

SOGAP (1990) *Les Etrangers sur le Marche Foncier Rural 1989 en Garonne-Périgord*, Société d'Aménagement Foncier et d'Etablissement Rural de Garonne-Périgord, Montauban

Salt, J. (1986) International migration: a spatial theoretical approach, in M. Pacione (ed.) *Population Geography*, Croom Helm, London, 166-193

Salt, J. and Clout, H.D. (1976) International labour migration: the sources of supply, in J. Salt and H.D. Clout (eds.) *Migration in Post-War Europe*, Oxford University Press, London, 126-167

Salt, J. and Kitching, R. (1992) The relationship between international and internal labour migration, in A.G. Champion and A.J. Fielding (eds.) *Migration Processes and Patterns Volume One*, Belhaven, London, 148-162

Savage, M., Barlow, J., Dickens, P. and Fielding, A.J. (1992) *Property, Bureaucracy and Culture: Middle Class Formation in Contemporary Britain*, Routledge, London

Scargill, I. (1983) *Urban France*, Croom Helm, London

Schrader, K. (1992) An old campaigner speaks out, *French Property News*, June, 17

Schwarzweller, H.K. and Brown, J.S. (1967) Social class origins, rural-urban migration and economic life chances, *Rural Sociology*, 32, 5-19

Short, J.R., Fleming, S. and Witt, S.J.G. (1986) *Housebuilding, Planning and Community Action*, Routledge and Kegan Paul, London

Shucksmith, M. (1983) Second homes: a framework for policy, *Town Planning Review*, 54, 175-193

Shucksmith, M. (1990) A theoretical perspective on rural housing: housing classes in rural Britain, *Sociologia Ruralis*, 30, 210-229

Silverman, M. (1992) *Deconstructing the Nation: Immigration, Racism and Citizenship in Modern France*, Routledge, London

Simmonot, P. (1991) *Ne m'Appelez Plus France*, Orban, Paris

Smithers, R. (1991) Caveat emptor, *The Guardian* (weekend section), 29 June, 38

Spittles, D. (1992) Squeezed between the gîtes, *The Observer*, 3 May, 56

Street, J. (1993) A house in France: the gîte man cometh, *French Property News*, May, 12

Sullivan, D.A. (1985) The ties that bind, *Research on Aging*, 7, 235-260

Sweeting, A. (1992) A Breton plot, *The Guardian*, 1 August, 26

Thomas, M. (1977) Cinq nouvelles résidences toutes les heures, *Espace 90*, 71, 3-14

Thompson, I.B. (1962) Economic transition in a high Alpine valley, *Tidjschrift voor Economische en Sociale Geografie*, 53, 215-217

Thompson, I.B. (1970) *Modern France*, Butterworth, London

Thrift, N.J. (1987) Manufacturing rural geography?, *Journal of Rural Studies*, 3, 77-81

Thrift, N.J. (1989) Images of social change, in C. Hamnett, L. McDowell and P. Sarre (eds.) *The Changing Social Structure*, Sage, London, 13-42

Troufleau, P. (1992) L'espace du logement en France, *Espace Géographique*, 21, 36-46

Valenzuela, M. (1993) Spain, in A.M. Williams and G. Shaw (eds.) *Tourism and Economic Development*, Belhaven, London, 40-60

Valero Escandell, J.R. (1992) *La Inmigración Extranjera en Alicante*, Instituto de Cultura Juan Gil-Albert, Alicante

Vartiainen, P. (1989) Counterurbanisation: a challenge for socio-theoretical geography, *Journal of Rural Studies*, 5, 217-225

Vining, D.R. and Pallone, R. (1982) Migration between core and peripheral regions, *Geoforum*, 13, 339-410

Warburton, S. (1992) Sound but slow return on gîte investment, *French Property News*, October, 6

Warnes, A.M. (1986) The residential mobility histories of parents and children, and relationships to present proximity and social integration, *Environment and Planning*, A18, 1581-1594

Warnes, A.M. (1991a) Migration to and seasonal residence in Spain of northern European elderly people, *European Journal of Gerontology*, 1(1), 53-60

Warnes, A.M. (1991b) London's population trends: metropolitan area or megalopolis?, in K. Hoggart and D.R. Green (eds.) *London: A New Metropolitan Geography*, Edward Arnold, London, 156-175

Warnes, A.M. (1993) Permanent and seasonal international migration: the prospects for Europe, in P. Hooimeijer, G.A. van der Knaap, J. van Weesup and R.I. Woods (eds.) *Population Dynamics in Europe*, Nederlandse Geografische Studies, Amsterdam, 68-80

Warnes, A.M. and Ford, R. (1993) The Changing Distribution of Elderly People: Great Britain 1981-1991. King's College London Department of Geography Occasional Paper 37

Webb, C. (1993) More than a year in Provence, *The Times*, 28 July, 31

Weber, F. (1982) Gens d'ici, émigrés, étrangers: conflits autour d'une chasse en montagne, *Etudes Rurales*, 87/88, 287-294

Weil, P. (1988) La politique française de l'immigration, *Pouvoirs*, 47, 45-60

White, P.E. (1986) International migration in the 1970s: revolution or evolution?, in A.M. Findlay and P.E. White (eds.)*West European Population Change*, Croom Helm, London, 50-80

Williams, R. (1973) *The Country and the City*, Chatto and Windus, London

Wisefile Ltd. (1992) *French Property News Survey*, London

World Tourism Organization (1990) *Yearbook of Tourism Statistics Volume Two*, Madrid

Wright, A. (1977) *The Spanish Economy 1959-76*, Macmillan, London

Wylie, L. (1966) *Chanzeaux: A Village in Anjou*, Harvard University Press, Cambridge

Wylie, L. (1974) *Village in the Vaucluse*, third edition, Harvard University Press, Cambridge

Yorke, T. (1993) Restoring the balance, *Living France*, 25, 21-24

Young, K. (1988) Rural prospects, in R. Jowell, S. Witherspoon and L. Brook (eds.) *British Social Attitudes: The Fifth Report*, Avebury, Aldershot, 155-174

Zlotnik, H. (1992) Empirical identification of international migration systems, in M.M. Kritz, L.L. Lim and H. Zlotnik (eds.) *International Migration Systems*, Clarendon, Oxford, 19-40